IN SEARCH OF PEACE

The Winners of the Nobel Peace Prize, 1901–1975

by
Edith Patterson Meyer
Illustrated by Billie Jean Osborne

Blessed are the peacemakers . . .

Matthew 5:9

Abingdon
Nashville

IN SEARCH OF PEACE

Manufactured in the United States of America

Library of Congress Cataloging in Publication Data

MEYER, EDITH PATTERSON.
  In search of peace.
  Includes index.
  SUMMARY: Presents information about the individuals and organizations who
have been recipients of the Nobel Peace Prize.
  1. Pacifists—Biography—Juvenile literature. 2. Nobel prizes—Juvenile litera-
ture. 3. Peace—Juvenile literature. [1. Pacifists. 2. Nobel prizes] I. Title.
JX1962.A2M42   327'.172'0922 [B]   77-24599

ISBN 0-687-18969-1

For my nieces and nephews:
Ruth and Elmo; Briant and Harriet;
John and Louise; Charlotte and Lewis;
Priscilla and Kenneth; Nancy and Ralph;
Emily and Lawrence; Esther and Jack

Acknowledgments and Sources

My thanks go to the staffs of the Ferguson Library, Stamford, Connecticut, and of the New York Public Library for their capable assistance.

Earlier chapters in the book rely heavily on my *Dynamite and Peace* (Little, Brown, 1958) and *Champions of Peace* (Little, Brown, 1959), both now out of print. Many books, magazines, and newspapers were consulted in researching them and also in researching *In Search of Peace*. A few of the most basic books are listed below.

The Author

Nobel and the Nobel Foundation: Falnes, Oscar J. *Norway and the Nobel Peace Prize* (Columbia, 1938); Halasz, Nicholas. *Nobel, A Biography of Alfred Nobel* (Orion, 1959); Lipsky, Mortimer. *Quest for Peace: The Story of The Nobel Award* (A. S. Barnes, 1966); Nobel Foundation, ed. *Nobel: the Man and His Prizes* (University of Oklahoma, 1951; rev. and enl. ed., Elsevier, 1962)

Dunant: Rich, Josephine. *Jean Henri Dunant* (Messner, 1956)

Suttner: Pauli, Herta. *Cry of the Heart* (Washburn, 1957); Suttner, Bertha von. *Memoirs,* 2 vols. (Ginn, 1910)

Roosevelt: Bishop, Joseph B. *Theodore Roosevelt and His Time.* 2 vols. (Scribner's, 1920)

Wilson: Baker, Ray Stannard. *Woodrow Wilson, Life and Letters* (Doubleday, 1927)

Nansen: Hall, Anna G. *Nansen* (Viking, 1940)

Butler: Butler, Nicholas Murray. *Across the Busy Years.* 2 vols. (Scribner's, 1940)

Addams: Linn, James Weber. *Jane Addams* (Appleton-Century, 1935)

Red Cross: Gall, Alice G. *In Peace and War* (Crowell, 1941)

Friends: Woodman, Charles M. *Quakers Find a Way* (Bobbs-Merrill, 1950)

Bunche: Kugelmass, J. Alvin. *Ralph J. Bunche, Fighter for Peace* (Messner, 1952)

Schweitzer: Gollomb, Joseph. *Albert Schweitzer* (Vanguard, 1949)

Pire: Houart, Victor. *The Open Heart* (Souvenir Press, Lond. 1959; Tapinger, N.Y.)

Luthuli: Luthuli, Albert. *Let My People Go!* (McGraw-Hill, 1962)

Hammarskjöld: Lash, Joseph P. *Dag Hammarskjöld: Custodian of the Brushfire Peace* (Doubleday, 1961)

King: Bennett, Lerone, Jr. *What Manner of Man?* (Johnson, 1968)

Brandt: Prittie, Terence. *Willy Brandt: Portrait of a Statesman* (Schocken, 1974)

Kissinger: Landau, David. *Kissinger: The Uses of Power* (Houghton Mifflin, 1972)

Sakharov: Sakarov, Andrei D. *Sakarov Speaks,* ed. and with a foreword by Harrison E. Salisbury (Knopf, 1974)

Contents

1. **A Remarkable Man and His Extraordinary Will**   **11**
   (Alfred Bernhard Nobel, 1833–1896)

2. **First to Be Honored**   **27**
   (Passy and Dunant; Ducommun and Gobat; Cremer; Institute of International Law)

3. **The Bypassed Baroness**   **42**
   (Bertha Kinsky von Suttner)

4. **Mediation, Arbitration, and International Law**   **51**
   (Theodore Roosevelt; Moneta and Renault; Arnoldson and Bajer; Beernaert and d'Estournelles; the Permanent International Bureau of Peace; Asser and Fried; Root; Lafontaine)

5. **Time Out for War**   **65**
   (International Committee of the Red Cross; Woodrow Wilson)

6. **"A Gleaming Hope" (The League of Nations)**   **74**
   (Bourgeois; Branting and Lange; Nansen; Dawes and

Chamberlain; Briand and Stresemann; Buisson and Quidde; Kellogg; Söderblom)

7. **International-Mindedness**   **91**
(Butler and Jane Addams; Angell)

8. **The Clouds of War Again**   **102**
(Henderson; Ossietzky; Saavedra Lamas; Cecil; Nansen International Office for Refugees; International Committee of the Red Cross; Hull; Emily Balch and Mott; Service Council of the British Society of Friends and American Friends Service Committee)

9. **New Problems, New Approaches**   **118**
(Orr; Bunche; Jouhaux)

10. **The Good Doctor of the Jungle**   **129**
(Albert Schweitzer)

11. **Reconstruction, Recovery, Reconciliation**   **139**
(Marshall; Office of the United Nations High Commissioner for

Refugees; Pearson; Pire; Noel-Baker; Luthuli)

12. **Crosscurrents in the Atomic Age** **155**
    (Hammarskjöld; Pauling; International Committee of the Red Cross and League of Red Cross Societies)

13. **Nonviolent Crusader for Social Justice** **167**
    (Martin Luther King, Jr.)

14. **Good Neighbors All** **176**
    (United Nations Children's Fund [UNICEF]; Cassin; International Labor Organization [ILO]; Borlaug; Brandt)

15. **"No Moratorium in the Quest for a Peaceful World"** **189**
    (Kissinger and Tho; MacBride and Sato; Sakharov)

16. **After Seventy-five Years** **201**

The Winners of the Nobel Peace Prize, 1901–1975 **204**

Index **207**

1. A Remarkable Man and His Extraordinary Will

(Alfred Bernhard Nobel, 1833–1896)

Every fall the announcement of the year's Nobel Peace Prize winners is an international event of outstanding importance. All around the world, people await with interest the names of those chosen to receive the coveted awards for their achievements in science, literature, economics (since 1968), and in the advancement of peace. Yet few know much about the man responsible for these prizes.

Alfred Bernhard Nobel was born in 1833 in Stockholm, Sweden, the third son of an inventor, Immanuel Nobel. When Alfred was nine, the family moved to St. Petersburg (now Leningrad), Russia, where the father had set up a factory that manufactured explosives. Alfred, though not as strong as his two brothers, was extremely bright and quickly became fluent in the Russian language. He also learned French and English, but his greatest interest was science, especially chemistry and physics.

The inventor father welcomed his sons, Robert, Ludwig, and Alfred, to his factory. He explained that the torpedoes and mines he manufactured were intended to protect cities and harbors from possible enemy attack, and he carefully showed them how they were made. He admitted that the work was dangerous, but "if you know what you are doing and keep your head, you'll be all right."

All three boys learned how to make explosives and, while they were still in their teens, Immanuel Nobel took the two oldest sons into his business. Sixteen-year-old Alfred, because of his facility with languages and his already remarkable scientific skill, was sent on a lengthy tour of

11

Europe to increase his knowledge and to gain ideas for improving the explosives manufactured at the Nobel factory.

Alfred visited several European countries, England, and even America, where he spent some months in New York City. Everywhere he met interesting people and gained important scientific ideas. By the time he returned to St. Petersburg, he was ready to experiment with some of them. Soaking gunpowder in nitric acid was one of his first successful experiments in the Nobel factory.

At this time the Russians were fighting the Crimean War and were glad to buy all the explosives the Nobel factory could produce. Alfred, along with his father and brothers, worked long hours, and this, added to the cold, damp climate of St. Petersburg, had a bad effect on his health, which had never been robust.

When the Russians lost the Crimean War, the army canceled all orders placed with the Nobel plant and refused to pay for back orders. Alfred was again sent to Europe, this time to try to raise money to keep the factory going. He was not successful. The plant closed, and as a result of the strenuous and disappointing journey, Alfred became seriously ill.

After his recovery, Alfred's father, mother, and youngest brother, Emil, who had been born after the move to Russia, went back to Stockholm. Alfred, Robert, and Ludwig stayed in Russia to wind up the Nobel business and try to make their own way in other fields. They found this difficult, and when their father urged Alfred to come to Stockholm to help him develop a powerful new explosive, he was glad to go.

In Stockholm, father and son worked together in their improvised home laboratory, experimenting with combining an explosive oil called nitroglycerine with different substances and in various proportions. Alfred, who was thirty now, finally developed an explosive that proved so successful when tested in a nearby stone quarry it was soon in demand as a blasting agent, not only in quarries, but also in the construction of roads and railroads. Alfred and his father were so encouraged that they set up a small workshop and began to manufacture ''Nobel blasting oil.'' They hired an assistant, a packer, and a delivery boy. Emil, a budding chemist, home from college for the summer, joined them. Things were looking better for the Nobels!

In September of 1864, Alfred was summoned home from a business call by a messenger almost speechless with fright. Instead of finding the prosperous little workshop, Alfred saw smoking ruins and the bodies of five persons, one of them Emil. The cause of the explosion was never known. Stunned, grief-stricken, and grim, Alfred made the necessary decisions and tried to comfort his parents.

This tragedy might have ended Alfred Nobel's work with powerful explosives, but it did not, because he was convinced that this highly specialized area of industrial science was his lifework. He was certain that explosives would play an important part in the construction of canals, tunnels, highways, and railroads; and he was sure that in their development he could make a major contribution to world progress.

When the Stockholm police forbade the manufacture of explosives within the city, Alfred set up a workshop on a barge on a nearby lake. There were many problems. Complaints from lakeside residents forced him to move the barge every few days. His father had had a stroke following the disaster and could no longer work. Money was scarce.

It was several months before Alfred was able to get together enough money to establish a small workshop outside the city. Then once again he began to fill orders. He himself supervised the slow and dangerous preparation of the nitroglycerine explosive, as well as the business. He also spent many hours trying to find a quicker, safer way to produce the powerful explosive, in spite of the severe headaches the nitroglycerine fumes gave him.

The Nobel product became so popular that the small

Swedish factory was overwhelmed with orders. So, too, were the factories Alfred opened in Norway and Finland. His keen business sense told him it was time to expand beyond the Scandinavian countries. First in Germany, and then in other European countries, Alfred Nobel established companies and factories. While in Italy, he met Professor Sobrero, the discoverer of nitroglycerine, who was pleased to hear that his discovery was being put to practical use and that all over the world the blasting oil was being used for constructive, useful purposes.

As people became familiar with the explosive, they grew careless in handling it. In late 1865 and early 1866, there was a succession of fatal accidents, including the blowing up of the factories in Germany and Norway. Nobel was in the United States, investigating patent-rights difficulties. He hurried back to Europe, and in the partially rebuilt German factory began working to find a way to make the nitroglycerine product safer. He worked almost constantly to locate some harmless substance to combine with the highly explosive nitroglycerine. At last he found a porous clay that would lessen the nitroglycerine's danger and yet not reduce its effectiveness. He tried combining the ingredients in different proportions and by different methods, and he tested and retested. When he was perfectly sure of the result, he put the new product on the market. He called it dynamite.

Powerful and comparatively safe, dynamite quickly became indispensable in mines and on engineering and construction projects. As the word *dynamite* became familiar, so did the name of *Alfred Nobel*. Before Immanuel Nobel's death, the Swedish Academy of Science presented the father and son jointly its award "for outstanding original work in the realm of art, literature, or science, or for important discoveries of practical value to mankind." Alfred Nobel cherished this award equally with the honorary degree of Doctor of Philosophy he received later from the Swedish University of Uppsala.

Nobel journeyed from one country to another to supervise the companies and factories he had set up. He was a shrewd businessman, but his first love continued to be scientific experimentation. Everywhere he went, he found his way into a laboratory. When someone asked him where his home was, he replied, "My home is where my work is—and I can work everywhere."

While this was true, Nobel realized he needed an established place of residence. In 1873, he bought a house in Paris, furnished it handsomely, and hired a corps of trained servants, though he rarely entertained. He had few close friends, but he knew many interesting people, some of whom he met through his membership in the Paris Swedish Club. When in Paris, Nobel spent most of his time and energy carrying on his business correspondence and working in his home laboratory. The nitroglycerine fumes still gave him bad headaches, forcing him to lie down frequently. When resting, he sometimes read literary works, including poetry, in any one of several languages. He would also relax by riding in his carriage through Paris parks and along the Seine.

Not satisfied with producing dynamite, Alfred Nobel developed an even more powerful explosive. First marketed in 1875, Nobel's "blasting gelatin" was later acknowledged to be the forerunner of TNT.

Through worldwide sales of his explosives, Nobel became extremely rich. Inevitably, this brought appeals for financial aid. Many of these were undeserving, but the inventor gave generously to the causes he considered worthy. He was especially interested in young people with scientific ability; often he would give them advice and occasionally would finance their education.

After a while Nobel began to feel that his elaborate Paris home was cold and impersonal. He missed the warmth of his childhood home and his mother's affection. Marriage did not seem to be the answer, for he knew his love of science would always come first. Thinking he might find a cultured, mature woman who would live in his home as a secretary-homemaker-hostess, he placed a carefully worded notice in a Vienna newspaper. In this notice he described himself as an elderly gentleman (he was forty-three).

An Austrian noblewoman responded. While it was clear that Countess Bertha Kinsky did not qualify either as a secretary or as a home manager, Nobel sensed that she was the kind of cultured woman he had envisioned living in his home, and he engaged her.

From their first meeting, Bertha Kinsky and Alfred Nobel found each other congenial. They conversed easily on world affairs, literature, even on their outlooks on many subjects. After a time Bertha, who was about ten years younger than Nobel, confessed why she had come to Paris. She was deeply in love with an Austrian nobleman, Artur von Suttner; but, though he loved her, his family disapproved of the romance because she was a few years older than he and because her family was penniless. Artur's mother had seen Mr. Nobel's notice in the paper and had urged Bertha to answer it, believing that with her at a distance, the romance would die.

The countess had been in Paris only a short time when a telegram from Artur announced: "I cannot live without you." Impulsively, Bertha left a note for Alfred Nobel and boarded the next train for Vienna, where the lovers were secretly married.

After Bertha left, Alfred Nobel devoted himself whole-heartedly to his scientific experimentation and business interests. When his brother Robert discovered oil in Baku on the Caspian Sea in southern Russia, Ludwig came to Paris to try to persuade Alfred to join him and Robert in developing the wells. Alfred refused, though he invested a considerable sum of money in the project. His life, he said, was already overloaded. Making important decisions, carrying on a heavy correspondence in several languages, consulting business associates, and journeying to distant factories already left him too little time to spend in the laboratory.

Yet Nobel's scientific experiments were so productive that patents were continually being taken out in his name. He acquired a larger laboratory outside Paris where he worked on projects intended for military use. This bothered Alfred, because he wanted his inventions to be used for constructive purposes. When he read of people involved in labor disputes being killed by dynamite bombs, and of high explosives becoming weapons of war, he asked himself if he were responsible for the way his inventions were being used.

Ten years after leaving Paris, the Countess Bertha Kinsky, now the Baroness von Suttner, returned with her husband to spend a winter holiday. Because they were both talented journalists and writers, Nobel took them one evening to a literary salon. There he noticed that Bertha seemed distressed by the casual way the guests talked of an impending war.

Nobel recalled this evening a few months after the von Suttners had returned to Vienna, when he received a book written by Bertha. *Die Waffennieder! (Lay Down Arms!)* particularly impressed him with its convincing descriptions of the horrors of war. His note congratulating the baroness on the book began a correspondence that dealt increasingly with the problems of war and peace.

Unexpected difficulties with the French government over Nobel's explosives experiments made it seem wise for him to look for another country in which to work. In 1891 he bought a villa at San Remo, on the Italian Riviera. Because of the mild climate, he could conduct year-round experiments outside on such things as rocket projectiles and various military devices. He also built and equipped a modern laboratory in order to experiment with making a variety of things from nitrocellulose. These products, intended largely for civilian use, included varnishes, dyes, and the forerunners of artificial silks and fabrics.

When Baroness von Suttner suggested that Nobel send a check to the Austrian Peace Society she had founded, he did so. At the same time he ventured to tell her that he believed the peace movement needed a practical plan more than it needed money, and he proceeded to propose one. It was simply that governments should agree to a year of arbitration before resorting to arms. In her reply, the baroness urged Alfred to attend the 1892 World's Peace Congress in Berne that August. Since Nobel was in Switzerland on business at that time, he did attend a session of the Congress, and he was impressed. He invited the von Suttners to visit him for a few days at the Zurich hotel where he was staying. During an afternoon sail (in an aluminum boat Nobel had invented) the von Suttners and Nobel discussed possible ways to bring peace to the world. Nobel wondered if the invention of some very terrible weapon of war might influence nations to turn to peace. He confessed that he thought the methods being proposed by peace organizations were too weak.

"If you knew the work was being well taken hold of, would you take a hand and help?" Bertha von Suttner asked him.

"Yes," replied Alfred. "I would. Inform me, convince me, and I will do something great for the movement."

Nobel's concern about war and peace was growing. He engaged a Turkish diplomat to approach various nations with his plan of international arbitration. This was a disappointing experience. After a year, when the man had accomplished nothing, Nobel dismissed him.

Nobel then had another idea. He wrote the baroness: "I should like to allot part of my fortune to the founding of a prize to be awarded every five years—say six times, for if we have failed in thirty years to reform the present system we shall inevitably fall back into barbarism. This prize would be awarded to the man or woman who had done the most to advance the idea of general peace in Europe." It would take time to bring about disarmament, or even compulsory arbitration, he admitted, but nations might be willing to bind themselves to take action against the first aggressor, and this would make wars impossible. "Even the most quarrelsome state would be forced to appeal to a court or else remain quiet."

Nobel's ideas did not particularly appeal to Baroness von Suttner. She wanted quicker, more positive action. Nobel, however, continued to think about the idea of a prize. He even made a will directing that half of his estate should be used to establish a special fund, the interest of which should be distributed each year "as a reward for the most important and original discoveries or intellectual achievements in the wide field of knowledge and progress," with particular consideration for persons who were "successful in word and deed in combating the peculiar prejudice still cherished by peoples and governments against the inauguration of a European peace tribunal."

Nobel began to yearn for Sweden, although his mother, his strongest bond with his native land, was no longer living. He bought property at Bofors, fifty miles from Stockholm, and established a laboratory-workshop there. To head it, he transferred Ragnar Sohlman, a capable young Swedish chemist, from the San Remo laboratory. He and Nobel had become true friends, with each man respecting, trusting, and liking the other. Nobel planned to begin experiments at San Remo, then have Sohlman go on with them in the larger Bofors laboratory, where Nobel would work with him during the summers. Near the Bofors laboratory, Nobel built a factory and engaged his nephew Hjalmar, Robert's son, as its manager.

Nobel was delighted to live for part of the year in his native Sweden. He maintained his Paris home, finding it a convenient stopping place on his journeys to England, Germany, and Sweden. In the fall of 1895, after a second productive summer at Bofors, Nobel spent two months in Paris. The diagnosis of a French doctor whom he consulted about frequent pains around his heart caused him to consider more seriously how he should dispose of his large fortune. The will he had made two years earlier no longer satisfied him. Instead of leaving money to his relatives, who did not need it and who would, he thought, be better off without it, he decided to leave his entire fortune to the encouragement of world progress and peace. Perhaps in this way he could accomplish something really splendid! Nobel wrote out in Swedish another will, had it witnessed, and sent it to a Stockholm bank for safekeeping.

After Nobel's return to San Remo, his heart condition forced him to take a complete rest. To occupy himself and forget his pain, Nobel resorted to his lifelong but neglected urge to write. He wrote a play which, according to the few friends who read it, was high-minded and idealistic but not very good.

With spring, Nobel's health improved. He began several projects in the San Remo laboratory, then traveled to Paris and London and on to Sweden to work in the Bofors laboratory for the third summer. He patented several military and civilian inventions; but, though productive, the summer was a sad one because of the death of his brother Robert. Ludwig, his other brother, had died earlier, and now Nobel was the only remaining member of his immediate family.

In Paris, on his way back to San Remo in the fall, Nobel's doctor diagnosed the heart trouble as hardening of the aorta and told him that he must slow down. Nobel found it amusing, as well as ironic, that he was ordered to take a medicine that, although called by a different name, was really nitroglycerine.

The warm sunshine and pleasant surroundings at San Remo made the inventor feel better. He worked in his laboratory and corresponded with Sohlman in Bofors about experiments on which they were collaborating. Early in December, however, Nobel became critically ill. His French and Italian servants put him to bed and summoned a doctor. Becoming delirious, Nobel spoke in Swedish, which none of them could understand. Telegrams were sent to Sohlman and to Nobel's two nephews, Hjalmar in Sweden and Emanuel in Russia. All three men left at once for San Remo. Emanuel arrived first, only to find he was too late. Earlier on the morning of December 10, Alfred Nobel had died.

Dr. Nathan Söderblom, pastor of the Swedish church in Paris and a good friend, traveled to San Remo where he conducted a short service. In his remarks he contrasted Alfred Nobel's public image as a rich and powerful man and his personal life of loneliness and suffering. Nobel, he said, had not been hardened by wealth or embittered by loneliness and suffering, and to the end remained warmhearted and kind.

Two weeks later a formal service was held in the ancient Stockholm church. It was followed by a solemn procession to the cemetery, where Alfred Nobel was buried beside his parents and brother Emil.

The following day the year-old will was opened at the Stockholm bank. The first surprise was that the executors of the former will—Nobel's oldest nephew, Emanuel, and an old friend—had been replaced by Ragnar Sohlman and Rudolf Lilljequist, a Swedish engineer and friend. Both were amazed at being chosen for this responsible task.

The contents of the will provided a greater surprise. After specifying a few minor gifts, it read (as translated from the Swedish):

"THE WHOLE OF MY REMAINING REALIZ-ABLE ESTATE SHALL BE DEALT WITH IN THE FOLLOWING WAY:

"The capital shall be invested by my executors in safe securities and shall constitute a fund, the interest on which shall be annually distributed in the form of prizes to those who, during the preceding year, shall have conferred the greatest benefit on mankind. The said interest shall be divided into five equal parts, which shall be apportioned as follows: one part to the person who shall have made the most important discovery or invention within the field of physics; one part to the person who shall have made the most important chemical discovery or improvement; one part to the person who shall have made the most important discovery within the domain of physiology or medicine; one part to the person who shall have produced in the field of literature the most outstanding work of an idealistic tendency; and one part to the person who shall have done the most or the best work for brotherhood among nations, for the abolition or reduction of standing armies and for the holding and promotion of peace congresses.

"The prizes for physics and chemistry shall be awarded by the Swedish Academy of Science; that for physiological or medical works by the Caroline Institute in Stockholm; that for literature by the Academy in Stockholm; and that for champions of peace by a committee of five persons to be elected by the Norwegian Storting. It is my express wish that in awarding the prizes no consideration whatever shall be given to the nationality of the candidates, so that the most worthy shall receive the prize, whether he be a Scandinavian or not."

                          ALFRED BERNHARD NOBEL
Paris, November 27, 1895

The nephews, Emanuel and Hjalmar, were bewildered at not being remembered in their uncle's will. Hjalmar, encouraged by his mother, brother, and sisters, angrily declared he would contest the will. Emanuel felt differently. Because he lived in Russia, he had met his uncle only a few times, but he had felt drawn to him and sympathetic toward his outlook on life. He recalled hearing his uncle say he would like to contribute to the progress of civilization and to bringing about a world of peace. Pondering this, and considering the enormous possibilities opened up by his uncle's plan, Emanuel became reconciled to the will.

The size of Alfred Nobel's fortune, approximately nine million dollars, created a sensation when it became known. So did his disregard of custom in ignoring relatives, friends, and Swedish institutions in favor of what many considered a crackbrained international scheme. Since science was Nobel's field and literature was known to be one of his great interests, the idea of creating prizes for achievements in these areas was understandable. But for the inventor of deadly explosives to endow a prize for peace seemed absolutely beyond reason! And to name the Norwegian Parliament as the selector of the peace prize winner, when for years Sweden and its neighbor, Norway, had not been on friendly terms, was considered outrageous.

The two executors of the will, Sohlman and Lilljequist, met for the first time a month after Alfred Nobel's death. They had no idea of the many problems they would encounter. They knew that first the country in which the will would be probated must be determined, since Nobel had residences in Sweden, France, and Italy. Then would come the conversion of the Nobel assets into "safe securities," and the creation of the fund mentioned in the will. There was also the unsettling prospect of Hjalmar Nobel's threat to break the will. Their first step was to engage an expert Swedish lawyer.

Regretfully, Sohlman abandoned his Bofors laboratory experiments in order to devote full time to executing the extraordinary will. Lilljequist, involved with building a new electrochemical factory, felt he could not leave Sweden, so Sohlman agreed to make the necessary trips to the other countries involved. He first went to Christiana, Norway, where he was glad to find that the Storting, Norway's Parliament, considered it an honor to have been selected by Nobel as administrator of the peace prize. It not only agreed to accept the responsibility, but quickly appointed a

five-member committee to attend to all matters connected
with the award.

Going to Paris, Sohlman engaged a French lawyer and a
notary to inventory Nobel's French assets. The contents of
the Paris house were sold at auction and the house put up for
sale. When he learned that Hjalmar Nobel was also in Paris,
working with lawyers in his attempt to break the will,
Sohlman rushed all movable assets out of the country in a
sort of cloak-and-dagger action. To his relief, a French
court concurred with the ruling of the Swedish court that
Nobel's legal residence was not France but Sweden. The
persistent Hjalmar then transferred his efforts to Germany
and England, but was unsuccessful.

From Paris, Sohlman went to England and arranged for
the handling of the Nobel French securities, now in a
London bank. Back in Stockholm, he was glad to learn that
the Swedish government had directed its attorney general
and the Swedish institutions named in the will to take the
necessary legal steps to put Nobel's "noble intentions into
effect." The Caroline Institute and the Academy agreed to
be responsible for selecting recipients of the medical and
literary prizes; and the Academy of Sciences, after some
hestitation, agreed to administer the physics and chemistry
prizes.

So many international legal problems arose that the two
executors called the German, French, and English lawyers
they had engaged to Stockholm to confer with the Swedish
lawyers. The Nobel assets were distributed in eight
countries—Sweden, France, Germany, Italy, England,
Russia, Austria, and Norway—and the laws of each country
had to be complied with. The jointly owned Baku oil shares
presented such a complicated problem that Sohlman went to
St. Petersburg to consult with Emanuel Nobel.

The two men liked each other, and Sohlman was pleased
that the other members of the Russian branch of the Nobel
family agreed with Emanuel that his uncle's idealistic plan
should be put ahead of personal profit. In contrast, the

Swedish branch of the family, headed by Hjalmar Nobel, continued to fight for what they considered to be their rightful share of the Nobel estate. They were upheld in this by the Swedish king, who mistrusted what he thought was the impractical idealism of the will and who especially disliked Norway's having a part in it. Emanuel Nobel ventured to suggest to the king that it might be embarrassing in future years for the Hjalmar Nobel family to be reproached by prize recipients for having appropriated funds that properly belonged to them. Finally, Emanuel Nobel and Ragnar Sohlman were able to persuade the Swedish Nobels to drop their suit in return for various concessions, including a year's interest on the Nobel estate.

It took nearly a year to accomplish the enormous job of listing and evaluating Alfred Nobel's assets in eight countries. Officials of the three Swedish institutions mentioned in the will then met to decide the best way to handle the huge amount of money now made available for the prize fund. They agreed to form an organization to be named the Nobel Foundation to manage everything connected with the fund except the selection of the prize winners. This would be left to committees to be named by the three Swedish institutions and, for the peace prize, by the Norwegian Parliament. Three fourths of the interest from the Nobel fund would be awarded to the prize winners, and one fourth would be retained by the Foundation to cover administrative costs. If in some years no award was made, the prize money would go back into the main fund. Prizes, however, must be awarded at least once every five years.

Representatives of the institutions involved set up a five-member committee whose president was chosen by the Swedish government. Each institution had three trustees; the Academy had six, since it awarded two prizes. Each institution could also establish an institute to investigate possible winners.

As other countries sang the praises of Alfred Nobel's generous deed, Swedes began to take pride in the fact that

the famous person was one of them. Their pride mounted as they read in a leading Swedish paper that this gift to humanity, "intended to further its development and promote its progress, as well as to serve purely idealistic purposes, was probably the most magnificent one of its kind that a private person has ever had both the desire and the ability to make." Still the Swedes resented Norway's right to choose the peace prize winner.

Nor was the Norwegian Nobel Peace Prize Committee, appointed by the Norwegian Parliament, happy about being dictated to by the Swedish Nobel Foundation. To overcome these objections, it was written into the Foundation statutes that Norway should make its own rules on all matters relating to the Nobel Peace Prize. The Norwegian Committee immediately appointed three advisers—one an expert on international law, one on sociology, and one on political history—to assist in the investigation of peace prize candidates. It also established an institute to help select the winners and to become a "peace laboratory, a breeding-place of ideas and plans for the improvement and development of international relations." This institute was to be housed in a building containing offices, studies, an auditorium, and a well-stocked and well-administered library specializing in subjects related to peace.

By fall of 1901, both Norway and Sweden were prepared for the awarding of the first Nobel prizes. The candidates had been proposed, investigated, voted upon, selected, and notified. In Norway, a gold medallion had been designed by the noted Norwegian sculptor, Gustav Vigeland. On one side was a profile of Alfred Nobel with his birth and death dates; on the reverse was engraved the Latin phrase *Pro pace et fraternitate gentium*—"For peace and the brotherhood of people." The date was now set for the annual awarding of the science and literature prizes in Stockholm and of the peace prize in Christiana. It was to be December 10, the anniversary of Alfred Nobel's death.

1901-1904
2. First to Be Honored

On the fifth anniversary of Alfred Nobel's death, December 10, 1901, the Norwegian Nobel Committee awarded the first Nobel Peace Prize. (On the same day, the science and literature prizes were awarded in Sweden's capital, Stockholm.) In Christiana, Norway, members of the Norwegian Storting, diplomats, university professors, outstanding citizens, and representatives of the press filled the Parliament auditorium to witness the ceremony.

Following a short address by the Storting president, the Nobel Committee chairman announced that the first Nobel Peace Prize was to be divided between Frédéric Passy of France and Jean Henri Dunant of Switzerland. Mr. Dunant, he said, was unable to attend, but Mr. Passy was present. There was a round of applause as the seventy-nine-year-old gentleman stepped forward to receive the emblems of the Nobel Peace Price—the gold medal, a certificate of award, and a substantial check.

Frédéric Passy had spent much of his life promoting the cause of peace. Trained in law, he had served in government posts, worked as a journalist, and lectured widely on economic and social subjects. As a young man during the Crimean War he was impressed by the contrast between the sympathetic way people responded to the suffering caused by natural disasters and their indifference to the suffering caused by war. He organized and became secretary of the French League of Peace, with the aim to "make war on war." The French peace society grew in importance. It existed through the Franco-Prussian War of

27

1870, and later, with Passy as its president, its membership increased to many thousands.

As a member of the French Chamber of Deputies, Passy pressed for voluntary arbitration between nations. He gained backing for an arbitration treaty between France and the United States and lectured in its behalf.

Frédéric Passy and William Randal Cremer of England founded the Interparliamentary Union (of arbitration) in 1886. The French League of Peace, renamed the French Society for Arbitration among Nations, hosted the International Peace Congresses held in Paris in 1889 and 1890.

changed. Forgetting his Algerian land scheme, he traveled over Europe seeking influential backing for the new organization. The idea of treating wounded soldiers not as enemies, but as human beings in need of help, seemed to appeal to everyone. Encouraged, Dunant, on his own, wrote and had distributed a circular demanding government aid in transporting medical supplies and asking that neutral status be given those who helped the wounded. The Geneva committee members were annoyed that Dunant had done this without consulting them and demonstrated their feeling by slighting him at the conference called by the Permanent Committee.

Thirty-six delegates, representing fourteen European countries, attended this 1863 conference in Geneva. A representative from the United States, there unofficially, described the Civil War work of the United States Sanitary Commission. The next year, at a second conference, the historic Geneva Convention was worked out to provide rules of conduct regarding the wounded and prisoners of war, and a new organization was formed, to be known as the International Red Cross. In courtesy to its host nation, it adopted as its emblem the Swiss flag, reversing its red and white colors.

Dunant, completely absorbed by his idealistic program, traveled over Europe, trying to persuade governments to adopt the Convention rules. Suddenly, because he had neglected his business obligations, including his Algerian land project, he found himself bankrupt. In Geneva, bankruptcy was regarded so seriously that upon returning there, Dunant was shunned by friends and even by some members of his family. Not wanting to disgrace the Red Cross organization, he resigned as its secretary and fled to Paris. Napoleon III, hearing of his difficulty, offered him financial assistance, but Dunant proudly refused for fear it would look as if he were being paid for having founded the Red Cross.

Dunant lived in Paris for three years, barely supporting

himself by teaching, editing, and translating. He avoided former friends and lost his self-confidence. Then came the Franco-Prussian War, with the Germans laying siege to Paris. This jolted Dunant out of his solitary, self-pitying life. Gaining official protection for the French Red Cross, he worked day and night with its members. He organized a General Association of Citizens to prepare dressings for the wounded and collect warm clothing for the French soldiers on guard duty. Because as a Swiss citizen he had neutral status, the French Red Cross asked him to mediate for the exchange of prisoners. Carrying a white flag, Dunant crossed the enemy lines behind a trumpeter. He was suspected by the Germans—and with reason, for he helped men escape on his personal passport. More than once he was close to facing death before a firing squad.

Risking his life daily, Dunant became more truly alive than he had been for years. He began to meet with progressive Frenchmen, among them Frédéric Passy and Ferdinand de Lesseps, the Suez Canal engineer, to discuss such advanced ideas as the rehabilitation of prisoners of war, the training of soldiers for useful peacetime trades, and the setting up of international arbitration courts.

After the war Dunant went to England at the invitation of the Social Science Association to lecture on the peacetime support of the Red Cross, on helping prisoners of war, and on the abolishment of slavery. But Dunant was poor; he made few friends; he neglected his health and his appearance and fell again into self-pity. Retreating to a garret room, he kept himself alive by part-time jobs of writing, translating, teaching French, and even distributing humanitarian leaflets.

One of Dunant's brothers finally sent him enough money to return to Paris, where for a time he served as secretary of Passy's peace society. But he was a bitter, broken, humiliated man who longed for his native land, where he was unwelcome. At last Dunant went to the village of Heiden, in the German-speaking part of Switzerland, where he found a comfortable home in a clean, inexpensive, and friendly hospice. There he spent his days walking, reading, writing—reliving the past and envisioning some unrealistic future.

One day the children in the village school told their teacher of meeting an old gentleman wandering along a lonely road. The teacher, Herr Sonderegger, investigated and discovered that the children's chance acquaintance was the once-famous Jean Henri Dunant, founder of the International Red Cross. He and Dunant became friends. Though Dunant still suffered from a sense of persecution, the teacher said his face "radiates love, goodness, and distinction."

With Herr Sonderegger's help, Dunant now translated his *Souvenir de Solferino* into German, and together they organized a Red Cross chapter with Jean Henri Dunant as honorary chairman. The teacher informed the Red Cross officials in Geneva of Dunant's whereabouts, but they did not contact him. In 1895, however, a Swiss journalist happened upon Dunant and published the story of his encounter in many papers. Soon letters and gifts began to arrive for the once well-known man, including the welcome news that the dowager empress of Russia was granting him a pension. Baroness von Suttner invited him to write an article for her peace paper, which he did, and he wrote a long letter predicting the success of the peace conference soon to be held at The Hague.

In 1901, a telegram informed Dunant that he and his friend, Frédéric Passy, had been awarded the first Nobel Peace Prize. The honor, Dunant said, brought him "comfort and hope," since it created an obligation to keep alive the work he so strongly believed in. At last the Geneva Welfare Society, out of which the Red Cross had grown, broke its long silence and wrote him: "There is no man who more deserves this honor, for it was you, forty years ago, who set on foot the international organization for the relief of the wounded on the battlefield. Without you, the Red

Cross, the supreme achievement of the nineteenth century, would probably never have been undertaken.''

Dunant delegated Dr. Hans Daae to accept the award for him and directed that his share of the prize money be deposited in a Norwegian bank. It stayed there until his death nine years later when, in accordance with his will, it went to charity—half of it to be used in Norway, the other half in Switzerland.

A white marble monument was erected over Dunant's grave in Zurich. It bore the figure of a man kneeling to offer water to a dying soldier and the simple inscription: JEAN HENRI DUNANT, BORN 1828; DIED 1910. FOUNDER OF THE RED CROSS.

In 1902, the second Nobel Peace Prize was again divided. This time it went to Élie Ducommun and Charles Albert Gobat, both citizens of Switzerland.

Élie Ducommun was the first director of the Permanent International Bureau of Peace. This organization, authorized at the 1891 International Peace Congress, held in Rome, was set up in Berne, Switzerland, to work out details of the peace congresses, to provide information on the various peace organizations, and to promote contacts among them. Ducommun, serving without pay, built the bureau into a valuable institution. A council of nineteen men assisted him in planning the congresses, but Ducommun handled the correspondence, issued a bimonthly newssheet, and built up a library of peace publications, including international treaties and decisions related to peace. In addition, he lectured and wrote extensively in behalf of peace.

Charles Albert Gobat had not only practiced law, but had taught it at the Sorbonne in Paris. As a member of the Swiss Government Council, he had aided in getting Switzerland to use The Hague Tribunal, the Permanent Court of Arbitration established in 1899, to negotiate disputes among nations.

Gobat believed there was a need for a specialized agency to handle information on the legal and parliamentary aspects of peace, and he helped found the Interparliamentary Bureau of Peace. He took over the direction of the Permanent International Bureau of Peace when Ducommun died in 1906 and, like him, served without pay. He made the organization an even more vital force in the peace movement. During his entire life, Gobat was an energetic, sincere, and capable worker for peace.

Perhaps because there had been some criticism of the first two peace prizes' being divided, the third Nobel Peace Prize, awarded in 1903, went to a single individual, an Englishman. **William Randal Cremer** had been forced to leave school at the age of twelve because of poverty. After working in a shipyard, he was apprenticed to a carpenter in London and for thirty years he continued to work at the carpentry trade. He joined the union in protest against low wages and long hours. His vigorous campaign for a shorter (nine-hour) working day resulted in a lockout that lasted nearly a year. This caused so much suffering that Cremer concluded that arbitration would have been wiser and that "warfare between those who are dependent on each other is madness." Believing that international differences, as well as industrial ones, would be best settled by arbitration, he spent the rest of his life fighting for achieving social justice by peaceful means.

Cremer was a Quaker and despised war. To him, the connection between the fight to improve conditions for the laboring classes and the fight against war seemed perfectly clear. Surely no one could fail to see what a heavy financial burden was placed on the poor by excessive armaments.

While traveling about in England and Scotland making speeches and organizing groups in an effort to improve labor conditions, Cremer founded the Workingman's Peace Association and became its secretary. Later this first international workingman's organization became the International Arbitration League. In 1875, Cremer took fifty of its members to a meeting in Paris where, with a hundred French workmen, a peace committee was formed and an international conference scheduled to meet in Paris in three years' time.

Cremer could see that members of Parliament had far greater opportunities to work for peace and for the laboring classes. He determined to become a member of Parliament, and in spite of being a workingman, by the time he was in his fifties, he actually succeeded. Only eleven other

laboring-class men were seated in the House of Commons; now, with Cremer, they became known as the twelve apostles. All of them worked hard to bring about industrial reform and to improve the economic conditions of the working people. Cremer also tried to promote international peace. In spite of his opposition to the Boer War in the face of the strong national approval of it, he was one of the few reelected to his seat. Cremer was a member of Parliament from 1885 to 1895, and from 1900 to his death in 1908.

With Frédéric Passy and several members of the French

Chamber of Deputies and of the British Parliament, Cremer organized an international society of legislators called the Interparliamentary Union. But he worked almost alone to secure an arbitration treaty between the United States and Great Britain. He took a petition with the signatures of more than two hundred members of Parliament to Washington and presented it to President Cleveland, then traveled about the United States making speeches in support of the treaty. At the time, nothing seemed to result from his efforts, but later the United States Congress passed a resolution favoring arbitration treaties with foreign nations.

The awarding of the 1903 Nobel Peace Prize to William Randal Cremer met with great approval. Nor did it surprise anyone that he donated his check for forty thousand dollars to the cause of peace.

Five years later, Edward VII announced his intention to make Cremer a knight. Because he was a Quaker, Cremer refused the honor, for he would not wear the fancy court dress or carry a sword, as was customary at the knighting ceremony. The king, learning the reason for the unprecedented refusal, permitted Cremer to be knighted wearing a frock coat and without a sword. A few months later, Sir William died. It was said of him: "He left a record equal to that of any other man who has striven for peace."

The rules regulating the peace prize permitted an "artificial person," such as an organization or institution, to be eligible for the award. In 1904, for the first time, the award went to this type of recipient.

The *Institut de Droit International,* or **Institute of International Law,** was a private association of scholars who studied and codified international law. Founded in Belgium in 1873, it had gained such authority that its recommendations concerning matters such as citizenship, extradition, and property rights in wartime were incorporated in the statutes of many countries. The organization had established an academy with sixty active and sixty associate members who met to discuss possible solutions to international problems and to formulate ways to arbitrate international disputes.

In 1899, the *Institut* had helped Czar Nicholas II plan the first Hague Conference; its hope was to establish a world of law and order. All nations were invited to send delegates, and twenty-six of them did. For ten weeks, the Conference discussed subjects connected with war and peace and international relations. Although the Conference did not accomplish all the Russian ruler or the *Institut* hoped, it did establish rules for arbitration and for the humanizing of war.

One of the influential publications of the Institute of International Law was its regularly published *Revue*. Another was a handbook of rules to govern and humanize the conduct of war. The organization was responsible for having many previously unwritten and inexact laws codified, legislated, and placed on statute books. It was also influential in making the principle of arbitration more widely accepted.

1905
3. The Bypassed Baroness

(Bertha Kinsky von Suttner)

In 1905 the Nobel Peace Prize was awarded to the **Baroness Bertha von Suttner.**

No one had thought to notify the baroness of Alfred Nobel's death in December, 1896. She read of it in a Vienna newspaper and was saddened at what she called "the snapping of a twenty-year friendship."

The baroness remembered her first meeting with the inventor, so soon followed by her marriage to Artur von Suttner. At first they had lived romantically in the Russian Caucasus as guests of her friend, the princess of the region. Later, they had earned a scanty livelihood there, teaching languages and music to children of the nobility. Then the Russo-Turkish war had come, bringing to the von Suttners hardship and poverty and the horrors of war experienced close at hand.

Yet all this had not been a total disaster. Artur had discovered his ability to write acceptable war reports and descriptive articles for Austrian newspapers and German periodicals. His success had inspired Bertha to try her hand at writing, and soon she was producing marketable articles and stories. After nearly ten years Artur's family forgave him for his marriage and self-imposed exile and welcomed him and his wife back to Vienna, where they both continued their writing careers.

Bertha von Suttner recalled that upon her second contact with Alfred Nobel, he had taken her and Artur to a Paris literary salon, and that she had been greatly distressed at the casual way literary and political personages had talked about the possibility of war. Having seen war firsthand, she

could not think of it impersonally, and such callousness filled her with determination to work actively for peace. And so she had written *Die Waffen Nieder!*, the story of Martha, a young soldier's wife who, after suffering from war, had a change of mind about its glory.

The magazine that had published other stories by Bertha von Suttner returned the manuscript, explaining that many of their readers would be offended by the horrors she described. After other magazine publishers turned it down for the same reason, she sent it to her German book publisher. He suggested she change the title and let a statesman go over it to strike out the most objectionable parts. When she would not agree to this, he reluctantly printed it as it was.

To the publisher's and Bertha's surprise, the "warlike German public" received *Die Waffen Nieder!* enthusiastically. It became an overnight success, and it was translated into other languages and published in many countries. In English it was entitled *Lay Down Arms!*, was compared to *Uncle Tom's Cabin* and called a "novel of purpose." It was Alfred Nobel's letter congratulating Bertha on her book that began their years of correspondence dealing chiefly with the problems of war and peace.

Writing the book had caused the baroness to become deeply involved in the peace movement. She organized the Austrian Peace Society as a chapter of the International Peace Association and went as its delegate to the Peace Congress in Rome. There, standing before a large and distinguished audience, she spoke eloquently about the need for peace. After this experience, Baroness von Suttner was invited to lecture all over Europe. She also became the editor of a new monthly magazine devoted to peace; it was published in Berlin and called by the title of her book.

Reflecting on the twenty-year friendship between herself and Alfred Nobel, Bertha recalled his promise to "do something great for the movement" if she would "inform" and "convince" him. Had Alfred Nobel perhaps left a will authorizing fulfillment of his promise after his death? She wrote to the Austrian ambassador in Sweden, inquiring about Dr. Nobel's will. Very soon she received from him a copy of it. Reading it, she realized how great an influence she had had on his attitude toward war and peace.

While she waited impatiently for the will to be translated into action, the baroness publicly called it "magnificent," "a masterpiece of immeasurable significance." She wrote: "It has been openly declared to the world, not by an overexcited dreamer, but by an inventor of genius (an inventor of war materials into the bargain), that the brotherhood of nations, the diminution of armies, the promotion of Peace Congresses, belong to the things that signify most for the well-being of mankind." And she added joyfully that this great gesture would bring the cause of peace to the attention of governments and individuals everywhere.

The outbreak of the Spanish-American War in 1898 was a blow to Baroness von Suttner, but her spirits soared when she read that the Russian Czar Nicholas II was calling a conference of representatives of governments to consider ways to achieve world peace. "The event cannot be estimated highly enough," she wrote. "One of the most powerful of the rulers acknowledges the peace ideal, comes out as an opponent of militarism. From this time on the movement is incalculably nearer its goal." She found it hard to believe that some nations were increasing their stock of weapons at the same time they were accepting the czar's invitation to the peace conference. Or that, while sending a representative to the conference, the German Emperor William declared: "Peace will never be better assured than by a thoroughly drilled army ready for instant action."

The Russian-sponsored Peace Conference at The Hague in 1899 was a high point in Bertha von Suttner's life. She listened approvingly to the statements at the opening session: "The object of the Conference is to seek for means to put a limit to incessant armaments and alleviate the heavy distress that weighs on the nations. . . . The nations cherish a burning desire for peace. . . . We are responsible . . . for doing a profitable work in establishing methods of employing some of the means for securing peace. In the front rank of these means stand arbitration and mediation.''

The baroness and her husband attended almost every session of the ten-week-long conference, attended by nearly a hundred delegates from twenty-six countries. She was elated at the decision to establish a permanent international arbitration court at The Hague, but distressed at the many compromises made and the watering-down of noble ideas to suit the convenience of various governments.

"Peace Bertha," as the baroness began to be called, reported on the conference to large audiences in many European cities. She confessed, however, that she "did not have unqualified joy in the report." Attractive, animated, impeccably groomed, and modishly dressed, Baroness von Suttner made a striking appearance on the lecture platform and spoke effectively for the need for peace. Neither she nor her husband, whose advocacy of peace was equally sincere, cared at all that many considered it improper for a woman, especially a noblewoman, to speak in public.

The awarding of the first Nobel prizes interested Baron and Baroness von Suttner deeply. The baroness, in spite of her high regard for Jean Henri Dunant, did not approve of his being chosen as Nobel Peace Prize recipient. Her reason was that he had devoted his life to humanizing war rather than putting an end to it. "St. George rode forth to kill the dragon, not to trim his claws," she said. She thought Passy, "the oldest, the most deserving, and the most highly regarded of all pacifists," should have received the entire award. Secretly the baroness had longed to have this honor herself. She believed that Alfred Nobel would have wanted this and might even have intended it, but she kept her thoughts to herself and graciously congratulated the winners.

On the day of the awarding of the second Nobel Peace

Prize, in 1902, Baron Artur von Suttner died. For twenty-six years he had been Bertha's constant and devoted companion, "remaining in the background but giving the fullest support to her endeavors." Though his death ended the romance of her life, she went bravely on in her work for peace, as he had urged her to do. In her fifties, and vigorously healthy, the baroness lived alone in a Vienna apartment, having little social life or contact with relatives or former friends. She made a point of attending and taking part in the annual Peace Congresses. Twice the Interparliamentary Conference honored her, as did the Women's Congress when it met in Berlin.

In the fall of 1904, the baroness crossed the Atlantic for the first time to attend the Peace Congress held in Boston and then to lecture and travel. She called America a true New World, "exuberant in strength and glad of its daring," ahead of Europe in its women's progress, social movements, technical arts, popular education, democratic spirit, and comfortable manner of living. She was delighted to find great interest in the peace movement and happy about President Theodore Roosevelt's promise to make many treaties and to call a second Hague conference. "Universal peace is coming," she quoted him as saying; "it is certainly coming—step by step."

The next fall, while on an extensive lecture tour in Germany, the baroness was notified by the Norwegian Nobel Committee that she was to receive the 1905 Nobel Peace Prize. She was deeply moved. She had heard that her name had previously been considered—and bypassed, and this had hurt her. This year, although she did not know it, Emanuel Nobel and several others had approached the chairman of the Nobel Committee and urged that it reconsider the baroness "as a duty to Nobel's memory."

Happy to receive this accolade at last, Bertha von Suttner was also grateful that this time the award was not divided; she really had need of the prize money. Since her German lecture tour would not be over by December 10, she asked that the customary Nobel address be postponed until the following spring. As December 10 fell on a Sunday, with the Parliament not in session, the occasion was used to dedicate the newly completed Nobel Institute building, and the baroness was awarded the prize *in absentia.*

In the spring Bertha von Suttner delivered her Nobel lecture in Christiania. As always, her listeners were impressed by her arguments against war and by the depth of her feeling for peace. Arbitration, she said, should precede, rather than follow the use of force. The peace movement had become "a fight for a world outlook and a world order," and a United States of Europe was not an unreasonable goal. Her address ended with the optimistic statement: "Terrible warlike relapses may yet occur, but the future will confirm my faith: the peace of nations is on the way."

After receiving the Nobel award, the Baroness von Suttner was in even greater demand as a lecturer. She spoke frequently to groups of workers or students in and around Vienna and before larger audiences both in Austria and in neighboring European countries. She enjoyed travel and the stir and excitement of big cities. Much of her time, however, was filled with her writing, most of which was related to the peace movement. Her articles were published in periodicals in many countries, including America.

In 1907, the baroness attended the second Hague Conference and then reported on it. Nearly every year she went to the annual Peace Congress where, to her delight, her advice was sought and her diplomatic skill was found useful in reconciling differing factions and reducing tensions. She enjoyed being treated as a person of importance. "I am known everywhere!" she exclaimed happily when she received a letter from Peking.

The baroness went to America for the second time in 1912 to make a lecture tour, financed in part by the Carnegie Endowment for Peace. She traveled across the country, speaking before peace societies and large assemblies and being the guest of honor at innumerable luncheon and dinner meetings. Everywhere she was received enthusiastically; it was clear that her audiences liked this high-spirited Austrian noblewoman as well as what she had to say about the need for peace and the way she said it, with fluency, force, and sincerity. The baroness was pleased with their response and with the number of supporters recruited for the peace movement. And to her personal satisfaction, the Carnegie Endowment gave her a monthly pension that would free her from all financial worry for the rest of her life.

Back in Europe, Baroness von Suttner sensed the threat of war. Austrian military men railed at her, calling her a traitor to her country for writing and speaking so vigorously in behalf of peace. "It seems to me," she dared to write, "that the great European disaster is well on the way. . . . Surely so much stockpiled gunpowder will soon explode." The people of the United States, she was glad to note, were protesting against war. "It would be a dreadful blow," she wrote, "if the leaders of the New World should fall into the crimes and errors of the Old."

A faithful friend during the baroness' months of declining health and her final illness was her publisher and enthusiastic co-worker for peace, Alfred Fried. He could give her few encouraging words about the world situation, but he listened sympathetically to her impassioned pleas for peace. One of her last remarks, Fried reported, was: "Lay down your arms! Tell that to many, many people."

The very month after Bertha von Suttner's death, in June, 1914, World War I began, embroiling nation after nation, not excluding those of the New World. It was perhaps a blessing that she did not live to see it.

1906-1913
4. Mediation, Arbitration, and International Law

(Theodore Roosevelt; Moneta and Renault; Arnoldson and Bajer; Beernaert and d'Estournelles; the Permanent International Bureau of Peace; Asser and Fried; Root; Lafontaine)

In 1906, when **President Theodore Roosevelt** received the Nobel Peace Prize, peace societies both in America and in Europe protested. They pointed to Roosevelt's scorn of pacifists, to his advocacy of a strong army and a stronger navy, and quoted his words: "Speak softly and carry a big stick," and "It is only the warlike power of a civilized people that can give peace to the world." How, they asked, could the Nobel Committee reconcile its choice with Alfred Nobel's directive that the prize for peace go to the man or woman who had done most for the "abolition or reduction of standing armies"?

When Theodore Roosevelt became President of the United States in 1901, peace lovers had protested his belligerent nature and his support of militarism. To their relief, he proved to be a peaceful President with a lively interest in maintaining good relations with other nations. By bringing before the international court at The Hague the case of an old quarrel between the United States and Mexico, President Roosevelt directed world opinion toward arbitration and influenced other nations to use the court. Twenty-four international disputes were submitted to The

Hague Tribunal within a short time, and peace became the
serious concern of diplomats and statesmen.

In the second year of Roosevelt's presidency, a general
arbitration treaty among nine American republics was
signed; it was the first treaty of its kind for the United
States. A few months later, Argentina and Chile signed a
treaty agreeing to limit their armaments and, with Britain as
mediator, to arbitrate all future differences. As a symbol of
perpetual peace between them, the two nations set up at a
high point on the Argentine-Chilean border a gigantic
statue, Christ of the Andes. The next year, largely through
William Randal Cremer's efforts, England and France
signed a treaty binding them for five years to submit to The
Hague Tribunal "differences of a judicial nature which it
may not be possible to settle by means of diplomacy." At
an arbitration conference in Washington, called by President Roosevelt, a liberal treaty between the United States
and Great Britain was drawn up but, to the President's
disappointment, was not ratified by the Senate.

It was not his encouragement of arbitration, however, but
his success as mediator in ending the Russo-Japanese War
that earned Roosevelt the 1906 Nobel Peace Prize. Japan,
after unsuccessful attempts to halt by arbitration Russia's
eastward expansion in her search for an ice-free Pacific
port, resorted to war. To the surprise of many, the small but
well-prepared Japanese army and navy defeated the Russian
forces again and again, though never decisively. The
American Peace Society asked President Roosevelt to offer
his services as mediator, but Roosevelt refused to do this
unless the request came from one of the warring nations.
When Japan, after another naval victory, secretly asked him
to suggest mediation, he agreed and invited the two nations
to send representatives to open peace negotiations "not only
for their own sakes but in the interest of the whole civilized
world." To a friend Roosevelt wrote: "I have not an idea
whether I can or cannot get peace between Russia and
Japan. I have done my best. I have led the horses to water,

but Heaven only knows whether they will drink or start kicking one another beside the trough.''

In August, 1905, President Roosevelt welcomed envoys from Russia and Japan aboard the U.S.S. *Mayflower* anchored off Portsmouth, New Hampshire. At the opening luncheon, Roosevelt proposed a toast to the speedy achieving of a just and lasting peace, but arriving at agreement was neither speedy nor easy. For three weeks negotiations went on between the two sets of envoys, with Roosevelt guiding the proceedings at critical moments and proving himself a master at smoothing ruffled feathers and soothing injured pride.

When at last the Treaty of Portsmouth was signed, practically every government head, including the Mikado and the Czar, sent President Roosevelt a message of appreciation. So did nearly every peace society. All agreed that the mediation between Russia and Japan was not only important in itself, but that it provided an example for the future.

The next year, President Roosevelt was awarded the Nobel Peace Prize. Like Baroness von Suttner the previous year, he received his award *in absentia*. In acknowledging receiving the emblems of the award he wrote: ''The medal and diploma will be prized by me thruout my life, and by my children after my death.''

In 1907, the President was both praised and criticized for sending the United States battleship fleet around the world. Some, like Roosevelt, believed the show of strength would promote peace; others called it a warlike gesture. After its completion, however, nearly everyone considered the voyage a great success, and President Roosevelt called it ''the most important service that I rendered to peace.''

Roosevelt had intended to call a second Hague Peace Conference, but he yielded to Czar Nicholas, who, having convened the first one, wanted to issue the invitations to the second. This second Hague Peace Conference, held in 1907, was attended by delegates from fifty-four countries.

Among them, at the suggestion of the United States, were representatives from the South American republics. Besides revising previous agreements and setting up a new method of appointing judges to The Hague Tribunal, many loosely worded international laws were rewritten. Some delegates, including Baroness von Suttner, were disappointed that almost all the Conference actions were concerned with limiting rather than with ending war.

When Roosevelt left the presidency in 1908, he stated truthfully that during his seven-year administration "we were at absolute peace, and there was no nation in the world with whom a war cloud threatened, no nation in the world whom we had wronged or from whom we had anything to fear."

After spending a year in the African jungles, Roosevelt delivered the long-deferred Nobel lecture on May 5, 1910. He called it "The Peace of Righteousness." While peace, Roosevelt said, was important, justice and virtue were higher values. To bring about righteous peace he recommended the signing of more international treaties, the strengthening of The Hague Tribunal, mutual agreements to limit armaments, and the formation of a league of all civilized countries to act as a body, when necessary, to enforce peace.

In an effort to win the presidency, Roosevelt organized a third political party, calling it the Progressive Party. But he lost out to the Democratic candidate, Woodrow Wilson. The following year, 1913, Roosevelt made an exploratory trip through the jungles of South America. He followed to its source the Brazilian River of Doubt, which thereafter became known as the Roosevelt River or the *Rio Teodoro*. On his return to the United States, he wrote *African Game Trails, Brazilian Wilderness,* and many magazine articles.

With the German invasion of neutral Belgium in 1914, and especially after the sinking of the *Lusitania* in May, 1915, Roosevelt declared, "I am not a peace-at-any-price man." He opposed President Wilson's peace policy and lectured and wrote in a vigorous attempt to arouse America to take a more active part in the war. When at length Wilson and the Congress declared war against Germany, Roosevelt wanted to raise a volunteer division and command it overseas. He was bitterly disappointed when Congress refused him permission, but was proud that his four sons and a son-in-law were in the army. When his son Quentin was killed in an air battle at the front he wrote a friend: "His death is heartbreaking, but it would have been far worse if he had lived at the cost of the slightest failure to perform his duty."

Early in 1918, Roosevelt became ill with a tropical fever he had contracted in the Brazilian jungles. Hospitalized, he seemed to recover, but became ill again and, on January 6, 1919, died in his sleep. To his sons fighting in France the son temporarily invalided home cabled: "The Lion is Dead."

Each spring the Nobel Peace Prize Committee met to consider names submitted by the peace organizations, government officials, professors, and others entitled to nominate candidates for the award. In the fall they met again to select the winner. Once the announcement was made, the decision stood, without comment or explanation.

In 1907, after four single winners, the prize was again divided. It went to Ernesto Moneta, an Italian patriot, and Louis Renault, an eminent French lawyer.

As a young man, **Ernesto Moneta,** along with his four brothers, fought in Garibaldi's war to free Italy, and, when the war was won, remained in the Italian army for several years. Then, having had his fill of war, he left the army, became a journalist, an editor of a liberal Milan newspaper and of a journal devoted to international arbitration and disarmament. He also wrote a book about the Italian war of liberation. Deeply involved in the movement for world peace, Moneta founded the Lombardy Peace Society. After receiving, with Renault, the 1907 Nobel Peace Prize, he

continued to work actively for peace not only in his own area, but as one of the thirty-five members of the governing commission of the Permanent International Bureau of Peace.

Louis Renault, co-winner of the 1907 award, had taught law in a number of French institutions, including the Paris Sorbonne. He was one of the first members of the *Institut de Droit International.* As one of the early judges at the Permanent Court of Arbitration (The Hague Tribunal), he was selected to arbitrate a number of important international cases. His reputation grew, and he became known as a "truly distinguished man of the law." The French government, recognizing his ability, appointed him its representative at several international conferences. All his life Renault worked to encourage arbitration. He was also active in the International Red Cross and was largely responsible for enlarging the scope of its regulations and extending the Geneva Convention to apply to naval warfare.

Again, in 1908, the Nobel Peace Prize was divided. This time the recipients were two Scandinavians, Klas Pontus

Arnoldson of Sweden and Fredrik Bajer of Denmark. Because of **Klas Arnoldson's** support of Norwegian independence, this decision brought criticism from nationalistic Swedes. Norway, after nearly a century of submission to the Swedish crown, wanted its own national identity, and Arnoldson had worked to achieve this separation peacefully rather than by war.

Earlier, as a railway clerk, then as a newspaper man and publicist, Arnoldson had been deeply concerned about world peace. After his election to Parliament he worked for peace through arbitration. He also actively promoted religious liberty and equal rights for women.

Although **Fredrik Bajer** also had favored the separation of Sweden and Norway, the Swedes did not object so strongly to his receiving the 1908 award because he was not Swedish but Danish. A teacher and politician, Bajer worked hard to promote friendship and neutrality among the Scandinavian countries and was active in many peace organizations. Years before receiving the Nobel honor, he had helped establish the Permanent International Bureau of Peace and had been its first president. Like Arnoldson, Bajer advocated international arbitration and promoted such liberal causes as the emancipation of women.

In 1909, for the third successive year, the Nobel Committee announced a divided award. A Belgian lawyer, Auguste Beernaert, and a French diplomat, Baron Paul d'Estournelles, were named to receive the Nobel Peace Prize.

Auguste Beernaert had held important posts in the Belgian government. He had helped enact election reforms, including universal suffrage, and had been president of both the International Law Association and the Interparliamentary Union. He was the Belgian delegate at the 1899 and again at the 1907 Hague Conference. Some thought he had been less than wholehearted in his support of arbitration because of the Belgian government's problems in the

Congo. There was no doubt, however, about Beernaert's devotion to world peace or his sincere efforts to promote it.

The 1909 co-winner, the French **Baron Paul d'Estour-nelles,** was closely identified with the Interparliamentary Union. In his youth he had studied oriental languages and traveled widely in the East to prepare himself for diplomatic service. Like Beernaert, he had attended both Hague Conferences. In 1902, while in the United States on a speaking tour, he had urged President Theodore Roosevelt to make use of The Hague Tribunal. Many credited him with influencing the United States President to arbitrate his country's dispute with Mexico there and thus set an example for other nations. One of the baron's ambitions was to bring about a close relationship among European nations. To achieve this, he worked hard, both as an individual and as a representative of the French government. Not only in Europe, but in the world at large, Baron d'Estournelles labored continually to bring about lasting peace.

In 1910, for the second time, the Nobel Peace Prize Committee chose an institution to receive its award, honoring the **Permanent International Bureau of Peace.**

The Bureau had been authorized at the 1891 Rome Peace Congress and established later that year in Berne. Fredrik Bajer was its first president and Élie Ducommun the director. Largely through Ducommun's efforts, the Bureau had achieved worldwide usefulness and importance. Ducommun assembled a large collection of material about peace organizations and important individuals in the peace movement all over the world, and promoted the use of the Bureau's extensive bibliographies, its records of arbitration negotiations and peace treaties, and its informative publications.

The more or less honorary office of president was dropped in 1943, after having been held by Bajer and Henri Lafontaine. Ducommun served as director of the Bureau from its beginning until his death in 1906. Then for twenty

years Charles Albert Gobat served as director—like
Ducommun, without pay. The Bureau moved from Berne to
Geneva, a more convenient location, where it continued to
be an indispensable part of the peace movement. It was
largely supported by Switzerland and three Scandinavian
countries—Sweden, Denmark, and Norway.

Beyond a deep desire for peace, Tobias Asser and Alfred
Fried, the two winners of the 1911 Nobel Peace Prize,
seemed to have little in common. **Tobias Asser** was a Dutch
jurist and statesman. A graduate in law of the University of

Leyden, he became a professor of law at the University of
Amsterdam and was one of the founders of the *Institut de
Droit International*. He was a member of the Netherlands
Council of State, holding the distinguished post of Minister
of State. Asser's contribution to peace was in the field of
international private law. He persuaded the Netherlands
government to call several international conferences in
order to make much-needed reforms in this area, and during

a ten-year period presided over four such conferences. Asser was also the Netherlands delegate to many international gatherings, including the two Hague Conferences. In 1885, he worked on the neutralization of the Suez Canal, and in 1900 was appointed to The Hague Tribunal. The cause of arbitration had no more ardent or intelligent supporter than Tobias Asser.

Alfred Fried, co-winner of the 1911 Nobel Peace Prize, was a bookseller in Vienna, Austria, when Bertha von Suttner's book *Die Waffen Nider!* was published in 1889. He was much impressed by it. When he moved to Berlin to establish a small publishing house, he started a peace journal, which he persuaded Baroness von Suttner to edit. The journal, called after her book, became a periodical of importance and the official organ of the German Peace Society, founded by Fried, as well as of several other peace organizations.

After a few years in Berlin, Fried returned to Vienna, where he started another peace journal. He attended peace conferences regularly, reporting them in detail in German-language papers. He and Baroness von Suttner worked closely together on peace-promotion projects and, like her, Fried became a popular lecturer for the cause throughout Germany and Austria. As the baroness grew older, Fried increasingly took the lead at peace conferences, where he was recognized as "an uncompromising pacifist of outstanding intelligence."

A few years after receiving the Nobel Peace Prize, Fried was forced into exile because he opposed Austria's entrance into the First World War. During the war, he lived in Switzerland, but returned to Vienna shortly after it ended. He was bitterly disappointed by the Versailles peace treaty, which he felt simply ended the war "without establishing a true state of peace which would mark the end of wars once and for all time." It was Fried's belief that a peaceful world would come about only if existing sovereign nation states were replaced by an effective international organization.

In 1912, **Elihu Root** became the second American to receive the Nobel Peace Prize. For years Root had held important offices in the United States government. He served as Secretary of War, Secretary of State, and as senator from New York. He became widely known as a constructive statesman and during the Roosevelt administration played a large part in strengthening friendly relations between the United States and Latin American countries. He arranged Pan-American conferences and encouraged the establishment of a court of arbitration for Central American countries. Root negotiated no fewer than twenty-four treaties for the United States. His enthusiasm for international arbitration was also borne out by his serving as one of four American members of The Hague Tribunal. When

Andrew Carnegie founded and funded his ten-million-dollar Endowment for Peace in 1910, he appointed Elihu Root to be its top trustee.

Critics of Elihu Root's receiving the award contended that his actions were made in connection with his official duties and could not be credited to him personally. This criticism waned when Mr. Root helped plan the League of Nations, helped establish the Permanent Court of International Justice, and took an active part in the 1921 Washington Conference for the Limitation of Armaments.

Henri Lafontaine, the 1913 recipient of the Nobel Peace Prize was a Belgian lawyer and statesman. For forty years

Lafontaine was a Belgian senator, and during most of that time was president of the International Bureau of Peace. He wrote extensively on international law and was a strong advocate of arbitration. He founded a Belgian peace society and an international review, was co-founder of an international library for pacifist literature, and was partly responsible for a clearinghouse for international organizations. He also compiled a history of international arbitration, covering cases from 1794 to 1900.

After winning the award, Lafontaine continued his fight for peace as the Belgian delegate to the League of Nations. He protested aerial warfare and urged peace lovers everywhere to pledge themselves not to take up arms if their country should enter a war of aggression. A strong internationalist, he envisioned and proposed the creation of "a world school and university, a world library, an international auxiliary language, international offices for labor, trade, statistics, and immigration, an international parliament, an international court of justice, and a central monetary office."

1914-1919
5. Time Out for War

(International Committee of the Red Cross; Woodrow Wilson)

The First World War, beginning in the summer of 1914, discouraged peace lovers everywhere. Only two years earlier, at a conference in Geneva, Switzerland, they had pledged themselves to oppose any war of conquest and to urge its settlement by peaceful means. But when war came, most peacetime pledges were disregarded, and their makers stood more or less firmly behind their governments. Except for a few meetings in neutral countries, peace organizations became silent for the duration of the war. Members of English peace societies were told that they had "a duty to humanity, to watch for the first reasonable chance to end the war by United States mediation, and a duty to their country, to provide for the wounded and destitute ('we are not at war with individuals') and to be tolerant toward enemy nations in our midst."

The Nobel Institute, located in the neutral country of Norway, went on with its studies of peace under the leadership of Christian Lange. In 1914, for the first time since its beginning, the Nobel Peace Prize was not awarded. Many complained. "Failure to make the award," said one critic, "is a lost opportunity for talking up for peace. . . . They [the Nobel Peace Prizes] should be awarded especially when the international situation seems darkest—to help in supplying a beacon of hope for all mankind." But the Committee remained firm, and no Nobel Peace Prize was awarded in 1914, 1915, or 1916.

In 1917, the Nobel Committee voted to bestow the award on the *Comité International de la Croix-Rouge,* the **International Red Cross Committee.** From the outbreak

of the war, its members had worked tirelessly and effectively. They had put prisoners of war and their relatives in touch, inspected prisoner-of-war camps, aided interned aliens, and arranged for the exchange of wounded prisoners. This was possible because the Red Cross headquarters was located in neutral Switzerland.

Again, in 1918, the Nobel Committee did not award a prize. It looked as if the Nobel Peace Prize was to be omitted the following year also, but in December, 1920, the 1919 award was finally announced. The recipient was the United States President, Woodrow Wilson.

Thomas Woodrow Wilson had a passion for study, along with strong convictions and the courage to stand by them. Perhaps he had inherited these traits from his Scotch-Irish ancestors and from his father, who was a minister. As a young man, he read many books on the art of government and studied law with the intention of going into politics, where he felt he would have "a great opportunity for public service." Instead, he became a university professor and a writer of weighty articles on American history and politics. Because he was a good speaker, he was also in demand as a lecturer. When Wilson became president of Princeton University, he held determinedly to a program of making the college both more scholarly and more democratic.

New Jersey politicians, observing Wilson's energy, capacity for administration, and his wide knowledge of

government, invited him to run for Democratic governor of New Jersey. Wilson agreed, provided he would not be bound by any promises. He was an enthusiastic campaigner, won the governorship, and at the age of fifty-four began "the work for which nature had designed him and his studies prepared him—the conduct of public affairs in a democratic republic."

Woodrow Wilson "fairly shook New Jersey awake" with his progressive program. Idealistic, yet cautious and mild-mannered, he was firm when convinced he was on the right course. In 1912, he was nominated as Democratic candidate for the presidency of the United States. People liked his clear-cut pledge to run the government openly and honestly, not for special-interest groups but for all the people. He was elected, and in his first term held his party together, prevented a war with Mexico, and as a "pledge of international good faith" extended several arbitration treaties negotiated by Elihu Root.

Two years after Wilson became President, the war in Europe brought a new set of problems to America. The country was divided: the isolationists felt that the European struggle did not concern America, and the interventionists believed it was America's duty to enter the war. With difficulty President Wilson steered a middle course, remaining neutral, but protesting sharply all violations of international law. If the United States could stay out of the war, he told the people, its influence would be greater when it was over and the time arrived for making peace.

When Wilson proposed a plan for "peace without victory," Germany replied by expanding her submarine warfare, torpedoing unarmed American ships, and threatening to help Mexico "recover" the southwestern states. Wilson broke off relations with Germany but still held back from taking the final step of war. He envisioned the frightful cost, the deaths of thousands of young men, sorrow in tens of thousands of homes, economic disaster, and disruption of peacetime life. But Americans were turning toward war, and more young men were volunteering to serve in the armies of the Allies or in overseas units of the Red Cross.

At last the President felt he must act. On the evening of April 2, 1917, he called a joint session of Congress and in a solemn voice announced the necessity for war. "The right is more precious than peace. . . . We will not choose the path of submission. . . . The world must be made safe for democracy." As he finished, the audience broke into cheers. The long months of tension were over; now a naturally active nation could get to work at the job of ending the war. Young men entered training camps; factories and shipyards increased their output; men and women bought liberty bonds; businessmen left their offices to serve the government as "dollar a year" men; women worked in munition factories; children planted gardens.

The first year the Americans were in the war was a dark one. The Russian alliance fell because of revolution at home; the Allies were hard pressed, and the Germans went from victory to victory. American peace groups tried unsuccessfully to find a "stable basis for peace." Woodrow Wilson studied their proposals and incorporated some in a plan of his own, which he made public in January, 1918. He called it the Fourteen Points. Eight of his points referred to specific national settlements; the others recommended open diplomacy, freedom of the seas, free trade, reduction of armaments, readjustment of colonial claims, and a league of nations to enforce the peace terms and prevent future wars. Wilson saw this league as "the key to peace," and gradually its establishment became his great ambition. During the early months of 1918, he repeatedly explained his Fourteen Points in newspapers and public addresses.

Toward the end of the summer of 1918, with two million American soldiers in France, the tide turned. Germany's allies stopped fighting; and Germany, with no more reinforcements, "neither of men nor of supplies nor of morale," neared the end of her rope.

The Allies, taken by surprise at Germany's feelers for

peace, did not have their peace program ready. Although England and France agreed in principle with Wilson's Fourteen Points, they were bound by secret treaties. At home Wilson's political enemies were urging a "realistic" peace, with heavy indemnities, in spite of Europe's being threatened by starvation and revolution.

Wilson held to his idealistic peace plan, and, to accomplish it, he determined to present his proposals in person at the Paris Peace Conference. He took with him dozens of experts, but unfortunately not a single senator or high-ranking Republican. As a result, the American delegation appeared partisan.

On his arrival in Europe in January, 1919, President Wilson was hailed with cheers and called a modern prince of peace. Before the Peace Conference opened, he toured the victorious countries, urging international friendship and the independence of peoples, and pleading for a league of nations to ensure lasting peace. The response was unbelievably enthusiastic. At this time, said Herbert Hoover, "Woodrow Wilson had reached the zenith of intellectual and spiritual leadership of the whole world."

At the Paris Peace Conference the "Big Four"— Britain's Lloyd George, Italy's Orlando, France's Clemenceau, and President Wilson—wrestled with the complex problems of a peace settlement. Wilson soon saw that his three counterparts still relied on secret treaties, military might, and political power, and that they put national advantage ahead of international justice. Step by step, he fought his way, meeting each objection with clear-cut logic. He worked practically alone, rejecting most of the advice of his American advisers. He insisted that German colonies be made mandates to be protected, not owned, by the Allies; that boundaries be redrawn according to ethnic lines, and that new nations be established on the principle of the "consent of the governed."

Wilson succeeded in writing into the peace treaty his beloved League of Nations, and he headed a committee detailed to draw up a constitution or "covenant" for it. After weeks of almost ceaseless work, he sailed home to present the peace treaty, including the League, to the Senate, where it must be approved before being adopted by the United States.

To Wilson's dismay, the Republican Senate would not accept the treaty. Not only did it insist on writing into it all sorts of restrictions, but it especially objected to the League. Such an organization, it feared, would lead to further European "entanglements." The President was forced to compromise. He took the revised document back to Paris, knowing that now the other powers also would insist on making changes. He was right. Many of the points previously conceded were reopened. Still Wilson fought on.

The revised peace treaty satisfied no one. The people of Europe, their hopes dashed, turned against Wilson. But it was Wilson, who, seeing his dream distorted almost out of recognition, was the most bitterly disappointed. The signing ceremony took place in the Versailles Palace Hall of Mirrors on June 28, 1919. The defeated Germans had no choice but to sign the treaty, though they complained that it was nothing like the Fourteen Points on which they had been told it would be based.

In the United States, opposition to the treaty grew, and so did the gap between the Senate and the President. Although it became clear that the Senate would never approve the Versailles Peace Treaty as long as the League of Nations was written into it, Wilson refused to give up the League. He knew that more than two thirds of the state governors and legislatures had come out for it, so he decided to go to the people and convince them that they should force their senators to approve the League of Nations.

By now, President Wilson's setbacks had affected him physically and he was suffering from almost intolerable headaches. Yet he traveled all the way to the West Coast and back as far as Colorado in his effort to persuade the American people to act in order to create a "new international order" of liberty and justice and lasting peace. The President had never spoken so eloquently, but it was in vain. America, sold on the "America first" slogan, wanted no part of Europe's problems.

The strain on the President was too great. He collapsed and had to be rushed back to Washington. He suffered a stroke and lay in bed, almost helpless, yet determined to live to fight for his precious League. But it was hopeless. The Senate never approved American membership in the League of Nations, although later it made separate peace treaties with the enemy nations.

In recognition of Wilson's authorship of the League, he was given the honor of sending out the call for its first meeting. The League of Nations convened in Geneva, Switzerland, in February, 1920, without American representation.

Somewhat recovered, the President partially resumed his official duties. He watched America, bent on a "return to normalcy," swing away from Europe. He could understand his countrymen's being weary with war and world problems, and he tried to believe that eventually they would wake up to their world responsibilities.

The Nobel Peace Prize Committee, in announcing the belated awarding of the 1919 prize to Woodrow Wilson, recognized his devotion to the cause of peace and his valiant efforts to bring the League of Nations into being. Wilson was far too feeble to go to Norway to accept the award and deliver the customary lecture. Many lectures on peace, however, could have been gathered from his speeches over the years.

On March 4, 1921, President Wilson forced himself to go through the ceremony of accompanying his successor, Warren Gamaliel Harding, from the White House to the Capitol. This was just about his last public appearance. Many pitied this man who saw the failure of his dream. A strong League of Nations, with America an active member, might have been Wilson's supreme achievement. That this goal was not reached was partly owing to his own shortcomings: his dislike of compromise, his partisanship, his lack of diplomacy, and his personal pettiness. Much more, however, it was because of the American people's failure to understand Woodrow Wilson's "glorious vision of peace and democracy."

Yet the dream was not entirely unrealized. The League of Nations did materialize, and the world did begin to recognize the right of peoples to political independence. Though America might turn her back on Europe for a time, Wilson had awakened her to a consciousness of the new international era with its interdependence of nations, its world responsibilities, and the necessity for world-mindedness. As he said, "The world has been faced toward peace and it will not turn back."

Woodrow Wilson died early in 1924. In the stone of his tomb in the Washington Cathedral is carved a crusader's sword.

1920-1930
6. "A Gleaming Hope" (The League of Nations)

(Bourgeois; Branting and Lange; Nansen; Dawes and Chamberlain; Briand and Stresemann; Buisson and Quidde; Kellogg; Söderblom)

Leon Bourgeois, an experienced French statesman and a strong internationalist, was the 1920 Nobel Peace Prize winner. Trained as a lawyer, he had been a delegate to both Hague Conferences and a member of The Hague Tribunal. He was president of the French Association for the Society of Nations, and had written a book, *Solidarité,* to explain his ideas on how to achieve and maintain ''solidarity'' among nations. In 1917, Bourgeois had headed a commission appointed by the French government to study the creation of a *Societé des Nations,* then abandoned this idea to give his full support to the League of Nations.

As a member of the Paris Peace Conference committee charged with drafting the covenant of the League of Nations, Bourgeois opposed his countryman Clemenceau's policy of power politics and supported the committee chairman, Woodrow Wilson, in his fight for an idealistic League. The French government made Bourgeois its first permanent delegate to the League of Nations in Geneva. He presided at its first meeting in 1920, and was a member of its first Council.

Difficult problems confronted the League of Nations. Bourgeois and the other devoted delegates had to contend with widespread doubts about the League and with national

legacies of suspicion and hate. In addition, the absence of the United States was a serious handicap.

The Nobel Peace Prize of 1921 was divided. As in 1908, it went to two Scandinavians, Hjalmar Branting of Sweden and Christian Lange of Norway. Both were delegates to the League of Nations.

After having been an astronomer at the Stockholm Observatory, **Hjalmar Branting** began a career in journalism. He became an editor, and then a statesman and a worker for peace. He was elected to represent the Social Democratic Party in the Swedish Parliament where he, like

Klas Arnoldson, worked for the peaceful separation of
Sweden and Norway. Branting also advocated general
suffrage and other liberal measures. He was a delegate to
the Paris Peace Conference and, on his return to Sweden,
persuaded his country to join the newly formed League of
Nations. He became his country's first permanent delegate
to the League and made many valuable contributions to its
deliberations. In his Nobel lecture Branting expressed his
lifelong belief in internationalism, saying: "The brotherhood of nations touches the deepest springs of man's
nature."

Christian Lange, co-winner of the 1921 Nobel Peace
Prize, also had worked for the separation of Sweden and
Norway by peaceful means. The Norwegian Parliament
appointed him to the first Nobel Peace Prize Committee and
he served as its first secretary. He was responsible for
creating the Norwegian Nobel Institute Library and for
making it an outstanding collection of materials related to
peace. Lange was a member of many international

organizations. As secretary of the Interparliamentary Union, he helped keep the Union alive by inviting its members to hold their meetings in Norway during World War I.

Lange, like Bertha von Suttner, believed in working to put an end to war rather than merely to humanize it. As a delegate to the League of Nations, he spoke up strongly in favor of disarmament. He also expressed his convictions freely at home. Lange believed that the Nobel Peace Prize should go only to a person who was truly outstanding in the struggle for peace, even if it meant making the award less frequently. Such a high honor, he felt, should not be given to someone "merely because he seemed the best of a meager herd."

Like Branting, Christian Lange spoke eloquently of internationalism in his Nobel lecture. He said he preferred the word internationalism to the word pacifism. To him, it was a more positive word, giving "a definite conception of how society should be organized."

Fridtjof Nansen, who received the 1922 Nobel Peace Prize, was a man beloved in his native country of Norway. "The Nobel Peace Prize," said a Danish journalist, "has in the course of the years been given to many different sorts of men. It has never been awarded to anyone who in such a short time has carried out such far-reaching *practical* peace work as Nansen."

Nansen had always been an out-of-doors man. As a young man he became intrigued with the strange ways of ocean currents and the almost unknown science of oceanography. An ocean current that would carry a piece of driftwood from the Siberian coast to the Arctic Ocean would also, Nansen reasoned, carry a ship. To test his theory, he eventually managed to finance the building of a stout little vessel he christened the *Fram (Forward)*. With a carefully chosen crew he started north in her; and for eighteen months

she was their home as, embedded in ice, the *Fram* was slowly carried westward by the current.

At the ship's nearest point to the North Pole, Nansen and a single companion left the *Fram* and made a dash for the Pole by dog sled. The southward drift of the ice slowed their progress so much that, with the dogs weakening and their food supply running low, the two men had to give up the idea of reaching the Pole. They built a snow shelter and holed up in it, existing through the long winter by eating the meat of the bears they killed. In the spring, they made their way south with difficulty and finally, to the joy of all, rejoined their shipmates on the *Fram*. Together they all sailed back to a great welcome in Norway. Nansen reported the unique adventure in *In Farthest North* and also in lectures he gave in Europe and in the United States.

Fridtjof Nansen became the first professor of oceanography at Christiania University. Though the life of scientific study on land and exploration at sea suited him perfectly, he left it to take part in the negotiations with Sweden for Norway's independence. When Sweden reluctantly agreed to Norwegian independence, and Norway invited Danish Prince Carl to become its king, Nansen was one of those who escorted him to his new kingdom.

The coming of World War I filled Fridtjof Nansen with horror. "The people of Europe, the 'torchbearers of civilization,' are devouring one another," he said, "trampling civilization underfoot, laying Europe in ruins, and who will be the gainer? For what are they fighting? Power—only for power."

Because the war made it impossible for Norway to import grain from the eastern European countries, Norway turned to the United States. This nation, now at war, was reluctant to sell to neutral Norway, so the Norwegian government appointed a commission, with Dr. Nansen at its head, to go to Washington to persuade the United States to sell the grain. After several months of patient negotiation this was accomplished, chiefly as a result of Nansen's diplomatic skill.

Nansen believed so strongly that the League of Nations was the best means of bringing about a better world that after the war he left his scientific work to represent Norway at the League's first Assembly. The League of Nations was facing a tremendous problem. Roughly ten million prisoners of war were existing in makeshift huts in Siberia or Turkestan. The Red Cross, the Society of Friends, the YMCA, and other humanitarian organizations had sent medicines, food, clothing, tools, and books. The League of Nations was asked to get the men back home. It requested Dr. Nansen to organize this venture. At first he refused,

then was persuaded to reconsider when he was told that he
need only give a short time to organizing the work and
getting it started.

When the Soviet Union, rejected by the League, refused
to deal with it, Nansen persuaded the Russians to work
through him with the nations involved. The Russian
government promised to bring home the Russian soldiers
who had been interned in central Europe and to provide two
trains a week to transport the prisoners in Siberia to its
western frontier.

Through an international loan, the League provided the
needed money for trainloads of supplies to be rushed to
Siberia. Nansen combined all the helping organizations into
one overall unit; he set up quarantines on frontiers to
prevent the spread of disease; he borrowed interned German
ships from England for use on the Atlantic and arranged for
the American Repatriation Committee to supply other ships
to carry returning prisoners across the Pacific. To
everyone's amazement, within the first six months Nansen
got a million and a half men home, and within another year
close to a half million more. Working together on this
tremendous international job eased the discord among
nations; it also raised the standing of the League of Nations.
To it and to Fridtjof Nansen, reunited families all over the
world were forever grateful.

In addition to the prisoners of war, hundreds of thousands
of civilians were stranded in alien countries without friends
or money. Again working through governments and
organizations, Nansen reestablished thousands of homeless
people. For those who came from countries that no longer
existed after the war, Nansen devised a simple identity card.
Known as the Nansen passport, it was honored by fifty-two
governments. Nansen took great care to place refugees in
whichever one of the forty-five countries agreeing to receive
refugees seemed the best suited to them.

While Nansen was still at work settling refugees, he was
called to come to the aid of people suffering from famine in

eastern Europe. He returned to Moscow and arranged with the Soviet government to provide headquarters for the reception and distribution of carloads of food. He tried to get the League of Nations to sponsor the project, but its delegates could not see that a famine in Russia should be a responsibility of the League.

Working with private organizations was slower and less efficient, but Nansen managed to organize the distribution of the relief food where it was most needed. Always the scientist, Nansen looked ahead and tried to eliminate the causes of famine by providing seed corn and agricultural machinery to ensure future harvests. In addition to food, the Nansen Relief also furnished medicines and educational materials.

Probably Nansen's most ambitious "good-neighbor" achievement, undertaken at the request of the League of Nations, was the transfer to Greece of more than a million Greeks who had been living unhappily in Turkish territory, and of half a million Turks from Greece back to Turkey. Nansen placed the returning Greeks in unsettled parts of Greece, where they could farm, grow grapes, raise tobacco, and work at skills they had learned in Turkey. By developing industries that were new to Greece, they became an asset to the country rather than a liability.

Another large-scale piece of rescue work Nansen undertook was the saving of the Armenians who had survived the Turkish massacres when, in the name of patriotism and religion, the Mohammedan Turks killed thousands of Christian Armenians. The western powers, occupied with the First World War, did little more than protest the massacres. At the Paris Peace Conference, the remaining Armenians were given, on paper, a grant of land; this did not prove to be of much help. Nansen tried to get aid for the betrayed Armenians at the League, but was unsuccessful. Unable to forget their distress, he collected private funds and did what he could by himself.

Fridtjof Nansen was in the midst of his rescue work when

he was awarded the 1922 Nobel Peace Prize. No one criticized the decision. Dr. Nansen's "deep sense of humanity" and his faith in "the deep current of human sympathy" were mentioned when he was presented with the medal, certificate, and check. Characteristically, Nansen used the entire amount, about thirty thousand dollars, to help Greek refugees and to set up in Russia agricultural stations where peasants could learn how to use modern farm machinery. In his Nobel address, Nansen urged going back "to the old primitive Christian virtue, the feeling of brotherhood, precisely that which Alfred Nobel regarded as the heart of everything." He spoke of his desire to return to his scientific work, but said, "I have a feeling that I have done so very little, and this great reward binds me fast to the work I have just begun."

At the League of Nations, Nansen continued to work for economic progress in Greece and for the admission of Germany to the League. Lecturing in America, he pleaded for the Armenians and for international friendship in general.

Still intrigued by the North Polar region, Nansen planned to take part in an expedition to the North Pole in the new dirigible, the *Graf Zeppelin*. But he did not live to fulfill this ambition. He had worn himself out trying to make a better world for others, and in 1930, his vigorous constitution rebelled. He fell ill and, after seeming to recover, worsened and suddenly died. "Seldom or never has the sorrow of a nation been so much a sorrow of love," said a friend of Fridtjof Nansen. "And it was more than a national grief. A whole world mourned."

Perhaps it was the high standard set by Nansen, added to Christian Lange's advice about waiting for a truly worthy recipient, that led the Nobel Peace Prize Committee to omit the award in 1923 and again in 1924. The world situation was confused. The borders specified by the Treaty of Versailles were proving unsatisfactory, and Germany could not pay the reparations required from it "for damages inflicted."

In 1923, when Germany defaulted on its payment, France and Belgium marched troops into the industrial Ruhr region of Germany. Their invasion only made matters worse. Within a year the German economy had collapsed amid wild inflation. The Allied Reparations Commission appointed two financial experts from each of the Allied nations to study the situation.

The two appointees from the United States were Charles G. Dawes, lawyer and banker and vice president under Calvin Coolidge, and Owen D. Young, a corporation executive. Mr. Dawes worked out a plan that was accepted by the Allied Reparations Commission and by Germany. The French and Belgian troops were to leave the Ruhr, reparations payments were reduced, the German national bank was reorganized, and Germany was to receive a loan, secured by the country's industrial assets. These methods of stabilizing the German financial situation succeeded in improving material matters and reducing European tension.

The Nobel Committee voted to award the 1925 Nobel Peace Prize jointly to the creator of the Dawes Plan, **Charles G. Dawes,** and to **Sir Joseph Austen Chamberlain,** a member of the British Parliament. As in the case of Woodrow Wilson, these 1925 winners were not announced until the following year, along with the 1926 recipients.

For years Sir Joseph had served in various posts in the British government. While Conservative leader of the House of Commons, he had conducted the diplomacy that led to a conference in 1925 in the little Italian town of Locarno. This resulted in the signing of the Locarno Pact, a document aimed at tying up the loose ends of the Versailles Treaty. It defined boundaries, provided for the admission of Germany to the League of Nations, and in general promoted reconciliation among the European nations.

Many people were disturbed that the Nobel Peace Prize

was awarded to Dawes, who had never attended a peace conference or worked for international accord, or spoken up for the reduction of armies. Others did not approve of the honor coming to Chamberlain, a "national politician thrust upon the world scene." The award was defended on the grounds that it was intended less to honor these men than to recognize the importance of the Dawes Plan and the Locarno Pact. Both were highly significant. Fridtjof Nansen had called the Dawes Plan "the first light in the darkness of postwar Europe"; and the Locarno Pact, "based on practical international politics," had been almost universally approved.

The 1926 award also was divided. Its recipients, Aristide Briand of France and Gustav Stresemann of Germany, had both been instrumental in bringing about the Locarno Pact.

Aristide Briand was the Premier of France. He was an advocate of internationalism, especially when it would prove beneficial to France. Briand believed the Locarno Pact would bring security to France as well as to Germany, and to a lesser degree to the whole of Europe. He had been the French representative to the 1921 Washington Conference to Limit Armaments; he was a firm supporter of the

League of Nations, had worked for the reconciliation of
France with Germany, and had promoted the admission of
Germany to the League. He also believed in, and worked
for, the establishment of a United States of Europe.

Gustav Stresemann was the Chancellor of Germany,
and was as devoted to Germany as Briand was to France.
The relationship between the two men, however, was

harmonious. Stresemann, like Briand, had worked for
postwar reconciliation between the two countries and for the
inclusion of Germany in the League of Nations. He had also
sponsored Germany's adoption of the Dawes Plan. Eager
for his country to regain a respected place in the world,
Stresemann looked both to the East and the West for
understanding. In spite of sometimes seemingly devious
motives, he was deeply concerned with achieving and
preserving world peace.

In 1927, the Nobel Peace Prize was divided for the third
consecutive year and, as in 1926, between a Frenchman and
a German.

Ferdinand Buisson, the Frenchman, was eighty-seven at the time he received the award. He had been active in peace work for many decades, winning the title of "the world's most

persistent pacifist." Sixty years earlier he had helped Frédéric Passy form his French peace society and in that same year, 1867, attended the first International Peace Congress. During his life, Buisson wrote literally thousands of articles and probably gave an equal number of speeches to promote the cause of peace. One of his major efforts had been to reconcile France and Germany after World War I. To this end he had lectured in both France and Germany. By profession, Buisson was an educator; he had been inspector and director of elementary education for France's Department of Education and had taught pedagogy at the Sorbonne.

Ludwig Quidde, the German recipient of the divided 1927 award, was a historian, a politician, a teacher of history at the University of Munich, and for some years editor of the *German Review of Historical Sciences.* He was

a longtime leader of the German peace movement. Before
World War I, Quidde had been imprisoned briefly because
of his political attacks on German imperialism and then,
because of his pacifist activities, was forced into exile.
During the war he lived in Switzerland, where he continued
to write and work for peace. After the war, Quidde returned
to Germany and was elected to the National Assembly.
There he argued against Germany's accepting the Treaty of
Versailles. Later he was arrested for accusing his country of
secretly arming in violation of it, but he was soon released.
He approved of the League of Nations and favored
Germany's entrance into it.

In 1928, the Nobel Peace Prize was not awarded.

In 1929, the award went to **Frank B. Kellogg,** an
American lawyer-statesman, though the decision was not
announced until late November, 1930. The award presum-
ably was made to recognize the Kellogg-Briand Pact, which
condemned "recourse to war for the solution of international controversies." Strangely, Kellogg, whose name it
bore, had not sponsored the treaty, though he had been
connected with it when he was U.S. Secretary of State. This
came about through a letter from Premier Briand stating that
France was willing to sign a pact with the United States
outlawing war between the two countries. Somehow this
offer was made public, and immediately was vigorously
promoted by Nicholas Murray Butler, the influential
president of Columbia University. The treaty was ratified by
the United States Senate and subsequently was accepted by
many other nations. Yet, Dr. Butler wrote later in great
distress, "No sooner had it been ratified by sixty-three
governments than at least half of them began arming for
war, under pretense of arming for defense, at a rate that had
never been equaled in all history." In ratifying the treaty the
United States Senate had specified that the treaty left the
nation free to engage in a war of self-defense. The pact,

according to Dr. Butler, had erred in containing no measures of enforcement.

Before going into politics, Frank Kellogg had made a reputation as a "trust-busting" lawyer. He had never made any claim to being a peace lover or an internationalist. But in the year he received the Nobel Peace Prize, he became a judge at The Hague Tribunal.

In 1930, the Nobel Peace Prize went to an entirely different sort of man. **Nathan Söderblom** was archbishop of Uppsala and Lutheran primate of Sweden. For years he

was professor of theology at the Swedish University of Uppsala. Earlier, when serving as pastor of the Swedish church in Paris, he had known Alfred Nobel, and in 1896 had officiated at his funeral.

All his life Archbishop Söderblom worked both for peace and for ecumenicalism. He helped found the German World Union for Churches for International Understanding, which was the forerunner of the World Council of Churches. During the First World War he tried without success to rally Christians to put an end to the war. He became so highly esteemed that he was sometimes called "the best-loved man in northern Europe." The Nobel Committee in its citation stated that Archbishop Söderblom had received the Nobel Peace Prize "for his labors for international peace."

1931-1933
7. International-Mindedness

(Butler and Jane Addams; Angell)

Two Americans—Nicholas Murray Butler, longtime president of Columbia University and an ardent internationalist, and Jane Addams, progressive social reformer—won the 1931 Nobel Peace Prize. Both were "international-minded," a term invented by Dr. Butler and defined by him as "the habit of regarding the nations of the civilized world as friendly and cooperative equals in spreading enlightenment and culture throughout the world."

Nicholas Murray Butler had become interested in European culture and politics while doing graduate work in European universities, and his interest continued during his entire life. While working to make Columbia one of the great universities of the world, he urged Americans to take their overseas responsibilities more seriously. He believed that no civilized nation could live in isolation, and he said "When private citizens and public officials look upon international obligations and international relations as the upright man looks upon his personal promises and personal relationships, the peace of the world will be secure."

Through correspondence and personal contacts, Dr. Butler kept in touch with important leaders, both in America and in Europe. Because he held no political office, they sometimes entrusted him with delicate missions. His frequent lectures and writings gave him a wide audience, not only in academic and governmental circles but with the general public.

In 1910, Dr. Butler persuaded the philanthropist Andrew Carnegie to donate ten million dollars to establish the Carnegie Endowment for International Peace. Mr. Carnegie chose Elihu Root, the 1912 Nobel Peace Prize winner, to head its board of trustees and Nicholas Murray Butler to develop its division for education and publicity. Dr. Butler quickly set up international-mind alcoves in public libraries and started lecture courses, international-relations clubs, conferences, and study programs.

To such a strong internationalist, the First World War came as a great shock. At first, Dr. Butler supported neutrality. Then, like most Americans, he became drawn into the conflict. But as soon as the war was over, he resumed his efforts to create an "enlightened sympathetic public opinion" toward international affairs. All through the twenties, in spite of the way the United States was pulling back from involvement in any European matter, Butler worked for the recognition of the "fundamental and controlling fact that the world today is an international world."

It was Butler's lectures and his open letter to the American public in support of the Kellogg-Briand treaty that "sold" isolationist-inclined America on this pact that renounced war as an "instrument of policy." And it was the public opinion Butler created that forced Secretary of State Kellogg and the United States Senate into action. The ratification of the Kellogg-Briand Pact by the United States and France was followed by that of practically all the world powers. But the treaty failed to achieve its end because it lacked the teeth to guarantee peace and left the door open to so-called wars of defense.

Dr. Butler believed that in a democracy it was the duty of every good citizen to work for better public administration, both national and local. While he preferred the life of an educator to that of a public official, he made his influence felt in his country's affairs. Every four years he was an official delegate to the Republican National Convention, where he took part in shaping the party's platform.

The selection of Nicholas Murray Butler as co-winner of the 1931 Nobel Peace Prize honored his lifelong work for internationalism, both personally and through the Carnegie

Endowment for International Peace. He was unable to go to Oslo (as Christiania was now called) for the December 10 ceremonies, and the award was accepted for him by the American minister to Norway.

For another ten years after receiving the great honor, Dr. Butler continued to work actively for international friendship and peace. Then, with increasing age and near blindness, he resigned the presidency of Columbia University, curtailed his vast correspondence, and gradually gave up his strenuous promotion of international-mindedness.

Jane Addams, co-winner of the 1931 Nobel Peace Prize and the first woman to receive this award since Bertha von Suttner in 1905, was called "the spokesman for all the peace-loving women of the world."

Miss Addams grew up in a small Illinois town and attended Rockport College. Afterward, she spent two years in Europe, "pursuing culture." But her most vivid impression was of a Saturday-night food auction in London where poor, hungry people reached for half-spoiled vegetables. She visited Toynbee Hall, which, purposely located in the most squalid section of London, was probably the world's first social settlement. Inspired by her visit, Jane Addams made up her mind that she too would live among the poor and serve them.

Because she believed that such service should be based on knowledge and understanding, Miss Addams spent several more years, some of them in Europe, preparing for her life's work. "The mere foothold of a house," she wrote, "easily accessible, ample in space, hospitable and tolerant in spirit, set in the midst of the large foreign colonies which so easily isolate themselves in American cities, would be in itself a serviceable thing." She chose the crowded immigrant section of Chicago, and in 1889, assisted by her friend Ellen Starr and a few social-minded, college-trained young people, she opened Hull House.

In this first settlement house in Chicago, the Irish, Jews, Germans, Bohemians, Greeks, Poles, and Italians of the neighborhood were welcomed. To their delight, Miss Addams could speak the language of some of them. There were sewing and cooking classes for the women, and a place to leave their babies when they went out to work. Children, coming first out of curiosity, joined reading, play-acting, and handicraft groups. Everyone in the neighborhood soon learned that at Hull House they had friends who would help them improve their way of life in the new country. They found here protection from unscrupulous persons who tried to take advantage of them because of their ignorance, and discovered that if Miss Addams could not solve a problem herself, she usually knew someone who could. Besides being a neighborhood home, Hull House became a clearinghouse for human needs. In granting Miss Addams the first honorary degree it had ever given a woman, Yale University cited her "common-sense method of bringing about social reform by building it up from the bottom."

Jane Addams tackled city problems with the same courage, graciousness, keenness of mind, and persistence she used so effectively at Hull House. Not only did she help bring about laws to improve working and home conditions of poorer citizens, she was responsible for such landmarks of social progress in America as the juvenile court and the Immigrants Protective League. Her concern for neighborhood and city naturally expanded into national and international activity. Believing that the same qualities essential at Hull House were needed in the wider arena, she worked for industrial improvement, social reforms, and woman suffrage in America, and for international friendship and world peace. Through her effective lecturing and writing, the name of Jane Addams became well-known.

At the 1907 National Peace Conference Miss Addams, representing the women of America, expressed her hope that nothing so primitive as war would ever again halt the upward march of civilization. She was shaken when in 1914, war broke out in Europe, but her convictions did not change. The Women's Peace Party, organized in Washington, made her its chairman, as did the National Peace Foundation, formed in Chicago. She also presided over an extraordinary international meeting of women at The Hague to protest settling international disputes by war. The women worked out a plan by which they believed the present war might be ended and future wars prevented. Their plan was to set up a mediation board of experts from neutral countries. Staying in session continuously, it would collect and evaluate mediation proposals and forward the best of them to the governments concerned.

Following the meeting, Miss Addams called on eight prime ministers, nine foreign ministers, and the Pope to try to interest them in this plan. She reported that the idea of continuous mediation was well received, provided the United States, then neutral, would take the lead. President Wilson, however, did not back the women's plan since he had one of his own. In December, 1916, he asked the belligerent nations to state their terms of ending the war, hoping in this way to bring about a negotiated peace. His effort failed.

The industrialist Henry Ford also had a plan to end the European war. He proposed sending influential Americans to Europe on a "peace ship" as a "sort of private commission for continuous mediation." Although she felt the peace ship's goals and methods had not been clearly enough defined, Jane Addams agreed to go. Just before the sailing date, however, she became seriously ill and was out of circulation for a year. To her regret, the peace-ship venture failed and, she felt, in failing harmed other peace movements.

Jane Addams stood nearly alone as she opposed the entrance of the United States into the First World War. She declared boldly, "That the United States has entered the war has not changed my views of the invalidity of war as a method of settlement of social problems a particle, and I can see no reason why one should not say what one believes in time of war as in time of peace." Such outspoken pacifism made the once-popular woman an outcast. She was dropped by clubs and organizations, shunned by former friends, abused by journalists. Yet she continued to express her convictions. She protested conscription and defended the rights of conscientious objectors. She supported wholeheartedly the government's food administration program and spoke before thousands of women, urging them to produce and conserve food in order to save the world from starvation.

In the spring of 1919, Jane Addams presided over the first postwar Women's Peace Congress, held in Switzerland. The Paris Peace Conference was going on, and the women expressed their regret that the proposed peace treaty did not follow more closely President Wilson's Fourteen Points. They suggested amendments, which Miss Addams herself took to the Paris Conference.

From Paris, traveling under the auspices of the American Friends Service Committee, she went into Germany, where she saw for herself the threat of widespread starvation. Back in the United States, Miss Addams urged Americans to send more food to the starving children of Europe. But Americans were still bitter toward Germany, and did not respond to her appeals. She was dismayed to see the wave of nationalism, isolationism, and self-righteousness sweeping over America. Imperfect though she considered the League of Nations to be, she was also deeply disappointed by America's rejection of it. "The world is not at peace," she wrote in her 1924 Christmas message, "nor is there enough active good will in it to accomplish the healing of the nations." One thing, however, delighted her—women had at last won the right to vote.

During the postwar years, Miss Addams presided over the meetings of the Women's Congress in Vienna, Washington, Dublin, and Prague. The creed of the sponsoring Women's League for Peace and Freedom, formerly known as the Women's Peace Party, was Jane Addams' own: "To unite women in all countries who are opposed to every kind of war, exploitation, and oppression, and to work for universal disarmament and for the solution of conflicts by the recognition of human solidarity, by conciliation and arbitration, by world cooperation and by the establishment of social, political and economical justice for all, without distinction of sex, race, class, or creed."

Hull House, with Jane Addams still its strong and shining light, continued to serve its changing neighborhood and city and to spread its influence to all corners of the globe. As

America once more moved toward internationalism, the shadows that had surrounded the pacifistic Jane Addams during wartime melted away and she became again Chicago's and America's acknowledged first citizen. She had done more to promote the real welfare of Chicago, said the mayor of that city, "than all our political organizations or public officials."

In 1929, a festive occasion marked the fortieth anniversary of Hull House, and the following year Miss Addams brought her earlier *Twenty Years at Hull House* up to date with the publication of *The Second Twenty Years at Hull House*. The 1931 Nobel Peace Prize brought to her increased worldwide recognition; it was the highest possible tribute to her lifelong devotion to the cause of peace. Because of illness, she was not able to make the journey to Oslo. The American Minister to Norway, accepting the award for her, heard her called "the foremost woman of her nation."

In March, 1935, Jane Addams was the guest of honor at a gala dinner in Washington. It celebrated the twenty-fifth anniversary of the founding of the Women's International League for Peace and Freedom and also Jane Addams' seventy-fifth birthday. Greetings came from all over the world. The press, in contrast to its attitude during the war years, wrote enthusiastically of Miss Addams' accomplishments in the areas of labor legislation, social betterment, and peace. It is pleasant to know that she read and heard these tributes, for within three weeks Jane Addams was dead.

A Nobel Peace Prize was not awarded in 1932, and the year 1933 went by without a winner being announced. Then, in December, 1934, the 1933 prize was belatedly awarded to **Sir Norman Angell.**

A lifelong worker for peace, Sir Norman had written a book, *The Great Illusion,* which was originally published in 1910 and in 1933 was republished in an enlarged and revised edition. In its first edition, *The Great Illusion* had sold more than two million copies, had been translated into twenty-two

languages, and had become the most talked-of book about war since Bertha von Suttner's *Die Waffen Nieder!* It was discussed by casual readers, analyzed by scholars, praised by pacifists, and denounced by the military.

The subtitle of the book, *A Study of the Relation of Military Power to National Advantage,* hinted at the nature of "the great illusion." The idea that war was profitable, the author contended, was untrue in the modern world of interdependent nations. Even a so-called winner was a loser, not only in terms of human life, but in terms of economic and general well-being. Cooperation, said Norman Angell, was rapidly replacing physical force as the most important factor in human affairs; it was cooperation that brought prosperity and progress. Yet, he lamented, wars would continue until people recognized their uselessness.

The 1910 publication of *The Great Illusion* had started a popular movement for international peace called Angellism, and had prompted the formation of many Norman Angell Leagues. Despite all this, the First World War took place. Norman Angell, while driving an ambulance on the western front, continued to think deeply about the causes of war and how to prevent its recurrence. He found in the Treaty of Versailles the seeds of another war; but the League of Nations, seeming to be based upon the principles of collective security, appealed to him, and he urged the hesitant United States to join it. He wrote many thoughtful articles on international politics, and in lectures, both in England and America, hammered away at the need for "a world philosophy and a world conscience."

In 1931, Norman Angell was knighted. Two years later he brought out the revision of *The Great Illusion*. In it he used current history to prove the validity of the points he had made in the earlier edition. The following year, he was given the delayed Nobel Peace Prize in recognition of his lifelong influence for peace.

Sir Norman continued to plead for a "community of nations" to replace outworn competitive nationalism. It could come, he said, if men and women would do more than agree passively as to the need for peace and would work with "political maturity" for an international community.

Even in his seventies, Sir Norman Angell continued promoting his "design for peace"—freedom and tolerance in international affairs and a world governed by reason and experience.

"He thinks that he failed," a journalist wrote in reviewing Norman Angell's autobiography, *After All*. "But no—there are millions who learned from him: 'We can still make a cosmos out of this chaos, by taking thought.'"

1934-1947
8. The Clouds of War Again

(Henderson; Ossietzky; Saavedra Lamas; Cecil; Nansen International Office for Refugees; International Committee of the Red Cross; Hull; Emily Balch and Mott; Service Council of the British Society of Friends and American Friends Service Committee)

On December 10, 1934, when Norman Angell received the delayed 1933 Nobel Peace Prize, **Arthur Henderson** was given the award for 1934.

From his early days, Henderson had been active in the labor union movement. He formed the Labor Party and became its chairman soon after being elected to the British Parliament in 1903. He occupied various posts in the government, among them that of foreign secretary. Although Henderson was not a pacifist, he was not in favor of large standing armies, believing they contributed to insecurity and fear and tended to bring about war.

In 1912, Arthur Henderson was made president of the World Disarmament Conference established by the League of Nations. The threat of war in Europe prevented its success, but did not hinder Henderson from pressing for disarmament. In his 1934 Nobel lecture, he expressed his belief in these words: "There is no greater human issue upon which hope concentrates than the cause of disarmament. There is no greater achievement to be realized than that of securing the world's peace." It was commented that Henderson fulfilled Nobel's requirement that the prize for peace should go "to the person who shall have done the

102

most or the best work . . . for the abolition or reduction of standing armies.'' Yet when the Second World War broke out in the summer of 1939, Arthur Henderson, like most of his associates in Parliament, gave his approval to England's entry into the war.

Again in 1935, the Nobel Peace Prize Committee postponed the announcement of its decision until the following year. This time the delay was caused by an extraordinary situation. **Carl von Ossietzky,** the leading candidate for the prize, was a prisoner in a Nazi concentration camp. The Norwegian Parliament, which appointed the Nobel Committee, wished to maintain Norway's status as a neutral country and did not want to antagonize Germany. German leaders, who had heard that Ossietzky was being considered for the prize, had warned Norway not to provoke the German people "by rewarding this traitor to our country."

As petitions for Ossietzky's favorable consideration continued to arrive, matters became tense. The situation was resolved when two Nobel Committee members who held positions with the government resigned from the Committee. The three remaining members then lost no time in announcing the award to Carl von Ossietzky. When the German minister to Norway protested, he was told, "The Norwegian government is in no way concerned. Kindly address yourself to the Nobel Committee."

One of the many congratulatory messages received in Oslo read: "All honor to the government of Norway and the Nobel Prize Committee! That government deserves the highest credit for refusing to bring any pressure to bear upon the committee." The German government, on the other hand, called the award "a brazen challenge and insult," and Führer Adolf Hitler declared that "acceptance of the Nobel prize is hereby forbidden to all Germans for all future time."

Carl von Ossietzky's offense was that he had spoken out against war. As a young man, after serving four years in the World War I German army, he determined he would devote his life to trying to make another war impossible. He became secretary of the German Peace Society and helped organize a "No More War" movement. As editor of a liberal weekly paper, Ossietzky continually urged the German people to create a progressive nation under civilian, not military, leadership. He wrote many articles on foreign policy and worked for Germany's admission to the League of Nations and for the rebuilding of a peaceful Europe. Like Quidde, the 1927 Nobel Peace Prize winner, Ossietzky

dared accuse Germany of secretly rearming after the First World War. "At Versailles," he wrote, "we gave our word; when pledges are made, they should be kept."

This was too much for Germany's military leaders. In order to silence this brilliant, peace-loving journalist, they accused him of making statements that created false impressions abroad. When they made him face trial as a traitor to his country, Ossietsky's friends urged him to leave the country. He refused, telling them, "If you wish to fight effectively against rottenness in a nation, you must do it on the inside." Ossietzky was sentenced to eighteen months in prison, but after seven months was released in a Christmas amnesty. He returned to his paper and made even sharper accusations against the military-minded government and stronger pleas for international good will. His freedom lasted only a few weeks; this time Hitler did not bother to make charges but threw the peace-seeking editor into prison.

For five years Ossietzky was shunted from jail to jail and from one concentration camp to another. Under cruel treatment, he grew weak and finally contracted tuberculosis. Pleas for his release were ignored, but when it was announced that in spite of German opposition he had won the 1935 Nobel Peace Prize, German government officials hastily moved him from his cell to a prison hospital.

A five-man Norwegian delegation called on Ossietzky to invite him to Oslo to receive the award. By then, however, he was far too ill to make the journey, even if the German government had permitted it. Ossietzky received his medal and certificate of award, but of the prize money, the German government retained a large amount to compensate itself for his board and lodging while he was in prisons and concentration camps; and a Berlin lawyer, given power of attorney, took the rest.

In bestowing the award on Ossietzky *in absentia,* the chairman of the Nobel Committee said: "Carl von Ossietzky is not only a symbol. He is something quite different and something more. He is a deed and he is a man." And one of the past winners of the prize wrote: "All of us have in some way or other tried to do something for the cause of peace, but we say that he has done more than any of us."

In 1936, the Nobel Peace Prize went to a South American for the first time. **Carlos Saavedra Lamas,** an Argentine lawyer, diplomat, and statesman, had presided over the 1936 session of the League of Nations Assembly and several international conferences. Acting as Argentina's foreign minister, Saavedra Lamas was responsible for the

agreement of South American republics not to recognize
any boundary changes obtained by the force of arms. He
drafted the anti-war pact that was adopted by many South
American countries, and also helped end the lengthy
Bolivia-Paraguay dispute over border territory. The Nobel
award recognized Saavedra Lamas' strong support of
Pan-Americanism and of the League of Nations, as well as
his valiant work for internationalism and peace.

The winner of the Nobel Peace Prize the following year,
1937, was **Lord Cecil,** properly Edgar Algernon Robert

Cecil, Viscount Cecil of Chelwood. At the start of World War I, this British noble had left his Conservative Party seat in Parliament to serve with the Red Cross at the front. What he saw, he wrote, "made me hate war even more bitterly than I had done before." At the Paris Peace Conference, he served on President Wilson's committee and aided in drafting the covenant of the League of Nations. At his insistence, it included not only war-preventive measures, but humanitarian, social, and economic programs.

To Lord Cecil "the effort to abolish war seemed the only political object worth while." This belief led him to resign

from the Conservative Party to devote himself, as president
of the British League of Nations Union, to promoting arms
reduction and international cooperation. He pleaded with
the League of Nations to achieve a "collaboration of the
community of nations to prevent the triumph of violence."
Its failure to accomplish this brought about the League's
tragic downfall. Because of Lord Cecil's long and
courageous struggle to establish a peaceful world, no one
questioned his being entitled to the Nobel Peace Prize.

The last award made before the outbreak of the Second
World War was in 1938. It went to a "nonperson"—the
Bureau Internationale Nansen pour les Refugés—in
English, the **Nansen International Office for Refugees.**
The League of Nations established this bureau in 1930,
shortly after Fridtjof Nansen's death. Its name was a tribute
to Nansen and his work as the League's High Commissioner
of Refugees. In its first few years, this agency helped
resettle more than eight hundred thousand refugees, most of
them Armenians, Jews, and Germans from the Saar Valley.
After transporting them to a new country, the bureau acted
as an informational clearinghouse and a reference center for
the relief agencies and institutions that cared for them. The
year after the award, the organization was discontinued, but
in 1943 its work was resumed by the United Nations Relief
and Rehabilitation Administration (UNRRA).

In 1939, the wartime curtain fell, and for five years—
1939 through 1943—the Nobel Peace Committee made no
awards.

As the war ended, in 1944, the Nobel Committee
announced its first postwar award—to the **International
Committee of the Red Cross.** Once before, during the First
World War (in 1917), this organization had been honored
with the Nobel Peace Prize for its humanitarian wartime
work.

Even before World War I, the red-and-white emblem of the Red Cross had been recognized by most of the civilized countries of the world, and Henri Dunant's dream of medical aid to wounded soldiers, regardless of nationality, had become a reality. Twenty-five distinguished Swiss citizens governed the International Committee of the Red Cross; its headquarters in Geneva acted as a clearinghouse for all international Red Cross activities. National societies were encouraged, but in time of war the Geneva office, because of its location in a neutral country, was responsible for coordinating and supervising all work at the front.

Between the two World Wars, the peacetime work of the Red Cross had expanded tremendously, with the American Red Cross and other national organizations aiding disaster victims, both in their own and other countries.

During the Second World War, the International Red Cross sent representatives into war areas where national-society workers would have been banned because of enemy hostility. One hundred and fifty men and women, selected for their good judgment, tact, and expertise, went to prison camps to make certain that the rules of the Geneva Convention were being followed; these specified acceptable treatment of prisoners, terms of exchange, and other procedures. After talking with a spokesman for the prisoners, the representative made a detailed inspection report, listing such needs as improvement in food, hospital care, shelter, or recreation. Copies of this report were sent to the International Red Cross headquarters, to the government of the country where the camp was located, and to the government of the country for which the prisoners had been fighting.

In the Geneva warehouses, volunteers worked at receiving, sorting, and sending to prisoners of war and internees food, medical supplies, clothing, and reading matter donated by the national organizations. Each week the United States government sent an eleven-pound package to every American prisoner in Europe, and every other week to each interned civilian. During World War II, over four thousand Red Cross volunteers handled more than forty million packages.

Other volunteers processed the nearly ten million cables and letters that came into the Geneva office each month. Information on prisoners of war, interned civilians, and other war-displaced persons was listed on twenty-three million cards. This vast card-index system was responsible for the return of thousands of prisoners of war to their units and for the reuniting of many separated families.

The IRC also supplied food and medicines to civilians near starvation by reason of crops being destroyed or going unharvested because of the war. In a single month, the IRC served a quarter of a million bowls of soup to hungry children in Greece. When ships of the Allied nations could not safely cross the oceans, the IRC established its own fleet and carried tons upon tons of food to starving Europeans in ships marked with giant red crosses.

All matters the national organizations could handle were gladly left to them. It was the American Red Cross that provided the medical units and ambulance teams to work under enemy fire, the entertainers who jolted endlessly from camp to camp to cheer the overseas soldiers, and the coffee-and-doughnut girls to give them a friendly send-off.

How Jean Henri Dunant, called impractical by many of his associates, would have rejoiced in these humanitarian activities that exceeded his most optimistic dreams! And how he would have applauded the awarding of the 1944 Nobel Peace Prize to the International Committee of the Red Cross!

Cordell Hull, winner of the 1945 Nobel Peace Prize, was the American Secretary of State during the Second World War. He helped bring about unity among the Allies, and after the war was influential in getting them to support a worldwide international organization devoted to the preser-

vation of international peace and security—the United
Nations. According to President Franklin Roosevelt, Cordell Hull was ''the one person in all the world who has done
the most to make this great plan for peace an effective
fact.''

Both in times of war and in times of peace, Hull's
international policy was one of ''constructive good will
toward nonagressive nations.'' He promoted Roosevelt's
good-neighbor policy with Latin America and was responsible for trade agreements and friendship pacts between the
United States and several South American nations.

The 1946 Nobel Peace Prize was divided between two Americans, Emily Balch and John R. Mott.

Emily Balch, a devoted friend of Jane Addams, followed her as the foremost leader of the women's peace movement. Miss Balch was head of the economics and sociology department of Wellesley College; she also served on the Massachusetts Minimum Wage Commission and drafted the first minimum-wage law.

An ardent pacifist, Miss Balch was a delegate to the International Congress of Women at The Hague in 1915.There she helped prepare the continuous-mediation plan for ending World War I, and after the conference visited Scandinavia and Russia to try to influence their political leaders to adopt the plan.

Between the two wars, Emily Balch, replacing Jane Addams as president of the Women's International League of Peace and Freedom, worked through this and other organizations for world peace. Her pacifistic attitude and her vigorous efforts to keep the United States out of World

War II resulted in her losing her Wellesley professorship.
After a time, however, her views changed somewhat, and
she conceded that the war had to be fought to defend and
preserve human rights.

Miss Balch went to Geneva to attend the International
Congress of Women and remained there for several years as
director of that organization. After the war, she returned to
her Wellesley home. She found that her earlier pacifistic
attitude had been forgiven, and when she opened her home
to refugees and other displaced persons, the townspeople
applauded. Emily Balch supported the League of Nations
and was disappointed that the United States did not join it.

Because of illness, Miss Balch was unable to receive the
award in Oslo on December 10, 1946. Her persistent fight
for peace and her unfailing courage were mentioned in the
tribute paid to her, and her accomplishments were called all
the more remarkable because her methods were ''so much
the quiet ways of friendly reason.''

John R. Mott, co-winner with Emily Balch of the 1946
Nobel Peace Prize, demonstrated organizational ability
while a student at Cornell University, where he founded the
Christian Student Union. From then on he was a leader in
interdenominational church movements. He believed
strongly in human welfare, internationalism, arbitration,
and racial equality. In 1915, Mott became general secretary
of the International Committee of the Young Men's
Christian Association. He supported the United States'
entry into the First World War and served as a welfare
worker with the Allied armies and with prisoners of war.
For this he was awarded the United States Distinguished
Service Medal. The Nobel Peace Prize recognized John
Mott's lifelong devotion to international good will and his
leadership in worldwide movements for the betterment of all.

''One hundred and forty thousand persons have won the
Nobel Peace Prize,'' an American newsweekly stated in

November, 1947. In this dramatic way the public learned that the award had gone jointly to the **American Friends Service Committee** and the **Service Council of the British Society of Friends.**

Friends, or Quakers, believing that war is caused by want, fear, intolerance, and hate, are certain it will disappear when these conditions are replaced by the spirit of love. They were among the first to speak out against slavery and for equal rights of women, prison reform, medical care for the insane, and good public education. The keynote of their religion is service.

The Service Council of the British Society of Friends, soon after its founding in 1850, tried to prevent the Crimean War. After that war began, they boldly sent a relief expedition to Russian ports bombarded by the British navy. From then on, the Council was an increasingly active humanitarian force. By the time the First World War began, the Friends were so favorably known for their merciful deeds that they were allowed to go almost anywhere to relieve the suffering of war victims.

The American Friends Service Committee was founded in 1917, much later than its British counterpart. In the First World War, Congress ruled that men who objected to going to war on religious grounds should be drafted into the army and then assigned to noncombat service. Many Friends, believing that even noncombat service aided the war effort, refused to obey the government order. As punishment, more than five hundred conscientious objectors were sentenced to hard labor, and often had to endure cruel treatment and bitter insults.

Dr. Rufus N. Jones, chairman of the newly organized Service Committee, finally persuaded President Wilson to allow the Friends Committee to deal with the conscientious objectors. It was soon evident that these men were not shirkers or cowards or afraid of hard, disagreeable, or dangerous work. An American Friends unit went to France to work with the War Victims Committee of the English

Friends and the American Red Cross. They rebuilt bombed hospitals, repaired roads under fire, cared for the wounded and diseased, worked in the fields, and fed the starving.

Men and women of other faiths worked with and contributed money to the American Friends Service Committee. Its overhead was small, because everything was done in the most economical way and most of the workers received no pay. After World War I, Americans entrusted the American Friends Service Committee with millions of dollars for the purchase and distribution of food, medicines, and clothing for starving Europeans.

During the Second World War, the American Congress allowed conscientious objectors to claim exemption from military service and instead to perform civilian jobs at work camps. There the conscientious objectors who were Friends paid for their food and accepted from the government only the bare barracks. Not all of the Friends' young men were conscientious objectors. The Society of Friends gave its members complete freedom to meet the war situation according to their individual consciences and treated them with the same respect whether they were fighting, serving in a medical unit, or working in a conscientious-objectors' camp.

In the days that followed World War II, Friends helped repair war damage and brightened the outlook for many thousands by their imaginative, constructive activities. In European cities plagued by scarcity of fuel, the American Friends Service Committee rented rooms and heated them so people could drop in and warm themselves. It supplied women with wool to knit sweaters and with used clothing to remake into serviceable garments, and provided men with pieces of leather to resole shoes.

Awarding the 1947 Nobel Peace Prize jointly to the American Friends Service Committee and the Service Council of the British Society of Friends was a gesture richly deserved. "These indefatigable Friends," commented an American journalist, "have quietly and persistently confronted strife and starvation with peace and mercy, pestilence and death with healing and life, the dehumanization of man with redemption and personal love."

1948-1951
9. New Problems, New Approaches

(Orr; Bunche; Jouhaux)

In 1948, the Nobel Peace Prize was not given.

In 1949, the Nobel Committee, in an interesting change of pattern, awarded the prize to a man who advanced the cause of peace in a new and different way.

John Boyd Orr—Sir John, for he was knighted in 1935—was neither a statesman nor a professional peace worker. He was a Scottish doctor who specialized in the rather new science of nutrition. While professor of agriculture at the University of Aberdeen, he prepared for the British government a study of nutrition and health entitled *Food, Health, and Income*. In it he made the startling statement that half the people of Great Britain could not afford a proper nutritional diet and that 10 percent of them actually suffered from malnutrition. This shocked the British; it also made Dr. Orr's name well-known.

The League of Nations appointed the nutritionist to a committee charged with investigating nutrition throughout the world. Sir John advocated solving the world's food problems by hugely increasing the production of grain and other essential crops. If nations would stop emphasizing armaments and instead emphasize nutrition, he said, the world would soon have continuing peace. While nations might disagree widely on political issues, Dr. Orr pointed out that they would never disagree on the need for freedom from hunger, nor refuse to work for it.

In his Nobel address, John Boyd Orr declared that if governments would devote a hundredth part of their war expenditures to a scientific drive for increased food

production, "within a few years the political issues which divide nations would become meaningless and the obstacles to peace disappear."

The same year he received the Nobel Peace Prize, 1949, John Boyd Orr was made a baron. Since he believed strongly in the establishment of a world government, Lord Orr was made president of the World Federalist Association. He was also president of the British Peace Council and of the World Peace Association.

It was believed that the Nobel Peace Prize Committee had planned to award the omitted 1948 Nobel Peace Prize to Count Folke Bernadotte, Swedish mediator in Palestine for the United Nations, but shortly before the announcement, Bernadotte was assassinated by terrorists. Two years later, **Ralph Johnson Bunche,** who became Acting Mediator in Palestine upon Count Bernadotte's death, was awarded the 1950 Nobel Peace Prize.

Doctor Bunche had been graduated from the University of California in Los Angeles with honors, and had then gone on to Harvard for graduate work in political science. For a time, he was assistant professor at Howard University in Washington, D.C. Then, through a social-science research fellowship, he was able to study at Northwestern University, the London School of Economics, and the University of Capetown, South Africa.

A black American, Ralph Bunche had a special interest in racial relationships and in colonial or non-self-governing peoples. While studying in South Africa, young Bunche visited a native tribe. After the elders had looked somewhat doubtfully at his western clothes and light-brown skin, they accepted him as a temporary member of the tribe. This permitted him to learn many significant things.

Bunche returned to Howard with a Ph.D. in political science from Harvard—the first black man to win this distinction. He quickly became a full professor, heading a new department in political science. Though he enjoyed teaching, he left Howard to serve in the U.S. Office of Strategic Services. There, during the Second World War, Bunche provided the chiefs of staff with information that helped them in their preparations for the American army's invasion of North Africa.

After two years, Bunche was transferred to the Department of State, where he was an advisor on the delicate colonial problems confronting the soon-to-be-formed United Nations. Secretary of State Cordell Hull and Dr. Bunche attended the preliminary conference at the

Washington estate of Dumbarton Oaks where representatives from Great Britain, China, the Soviet Union, and the United States met to draft a tentative charter for the United Nations. When they dealt with the section on colonial territories taken from the conquered countries after World War II, it was Ralph Bunche who wrote most of the paragraphs on government and economics and the rights of the governed peoples. At the San Francisco Conference, where the United Nations was created, there was less argument over this section than almost any other part of the proposed charter. Soon after the United Nations was set up,

Dr. Bunche became the director of the UN Department of Trusteeship and Non-Self-Governing Territories.

Although the UN had been successful in helping avert several small wars in Asia and Europe, it seemed about to fail in the Middle East, where it had been entrusted with fulfilling Britain's 1917 promise of a Jewish homeland in Palestine. Jews, moving into Palestine in large numbers, were passionately proud and defensive of their new homeland, while Arabs felt just as strongly about being displaced from the region they had long regarded as theirs. Ralph Bunche was a member of a special investigation commission sent by the UN to Palestine in June, 1947.

When the commission recommended the partition of Palestine into separate Jewish and Arab states, war broke out. After a UN-arranged truce failed, the United Nations appointed a mediator, the accomplished diplomat Count Folke Bernadotte of Sweden. Trygve Lie, Secretary General of the UN asked Dr. Bunche to go to Palestine as Count Bernadotte's aide and advisor.

Ralph Bunche immediately began an intensive study of the religious, territorial, political, and economic background of the Jews and Arabs. In Paris, he gave his lengthy memorandum to Count Bernadotte, who read it as they flew on to Palestine together. Though no two men could have seemed more different than the thin, suave, aristocratic Scandinavian diplomat and the stocky, industrious black American scholar, they had much in common. Both were men of integrity and good will, devoted to the United Nations and dedicated to their task of bringing peace to Palestine. They soon became firm friends.

It was time, they agreed, to turn the uneasy truce between the Jewish state of Israel and the seven neighboring Arab states into definite armistice agreements. Together, the Count and Dr. Bunche traveled about talking to leaders, both Israeli and Arab. Although their car carried the flag of the United Nations, they were fired upon more than once.

As the action dragged, the two mediators decided to try to

speed it up by moving the talks away from the center of turmoil. They invited the participants to meet on the peaceful Mediterranean island of Rhodes. When some of the leaders did not arrive, Count Bernadotte flew back to Palestine to round them up, asking Bunche to join him in Jerusalem a few days later.

But in Jerusalem, bullets fired by fanatical Jews killed Count Bernadotte and the dark-skinned French officer sitting in the car beside him, who had undoubtedly been mistaken for Ralph Bunche. Bunche heard the news when he arrived at the Jerusalem gate. He was stunned. Not only was Bernadotte's death a deep personal grief, it seemed also to knock the props from under the shaky beginnings of the armistice agreements.

UN Secretary General Lie put Bunche in charge of the negotiations, and in the midst of mounting tensions he hurried back to Rhodes. There he told the Arab and Israeli leaders gathered for the talks: "The lives of many people and indeed the peace of the Near East hang in the balance. The decisions you will be called upon to make . . . are momentous. You cannot afford to fail. You must succeed. I have faith that you will succeed."

At first the atmosphere was one of bitter hostility; some Arab representatives refused even to enter a room where there were Israelis. Acting Mediator Bunche set up committees, sometimes with not more than a single man from each side. They met in small rooms, with each committee considering only one point. Gradually, the groups were consolidated. Every day, sometimes several times a day, Bunche met with each group. He slept and ate little. He worked with every ounce of his energy, skill, and patience. His background in political science and his thorough knowledge of the situation were invaluable, but even more important were his innate understanding of and respect for the emotions involved.

In January, 1949, after nearly three months of almost continuous meetings and a twenty-hour final session, the

first of four formal armistice agreements was signed. It was
the Arabs who suggested that everyone stay over a day to
celebrate. In a relaxed and amiable atmosphere, Dr. Bunche
presented each delegate a memento of the historic
occasion—a piece of especially designed and marked
Rhodes pottery.

The armistice agreements brought prestige to the United
Nations. In meeting a major test, it had shown the world
that, to quote the *New York Times,* "where there is a
genuine will to negotiate, the achievement of international
peace and security is really possible."

After his return to New York, there were congratulatory
messages, medals, scrolls, and honorary degrees for
Mediator Bunche. In an unusual personal reference at a
dinner in his honor, Dr. Bunche listed his biases and his
beliefs. He admitted to biases against hate and intolerance,
racial and religious bigotry, and biases for peace and the
United Nations; he stated his belief in the essential goodness
of people, the ability of the United Nations to maintain a
peaceful world, and the certainty that no problem in human
relations is insoluble.

Dr. Bunche made an extensive speaking tour for the
United Nations. Everywhere he emphasized two beliefs:
that the United Nations is the world's greatest force and
only real hope for peace, and that peace is "everyone's
business." To young people, he stressed the responsibility
to make a secure and peaceful world by becoming
responsible citizens, alert and informed, never losing faith
in themselves or in people or in the democratic way of life.
Every act of brotherhood, he said, is a contribution to a
freer, more peaceful world.

In August, 1949, Dr. Bunche made his final report as
Acting Mediator in Palestine to the United Nations Security
Council. He would have enjoyed returning to teaching, or
having time to write, but his strong belief in the United
Nations and his desire to help make a world where people
"practice tolerance and live together as good neighbors"

made it almost inevitable that he remain with the UN.

Dr. Bunche was finishing a late lunch in the UN dining room one day in September, 1950, when his secretary came to his table. "Mr. Bunche," she said excitedly, "I have a surprise for you. You have won the Nobel Peace Prize!"

Ralph Bunche could hardly believe it, but soon telegrams and phone calls began to pour in, and men and women from all over the Secretariat arrived to congratulate him. The well-deserved honor made the United Nations very proud, said Secretary General Lie. To this, Ralph Bunche replied that if, as he suspected, the honor had come because of the success of the Palestine negotiation, it also belonged to Count Bernadotte, the UN observers, and the Security Council that supported them.

Black Americans were justifiably proud of the Nobel Committee's selection of Ralph Bunche. This was the first time a black person had won this high honor. A group of black American friends accompanied Dr. and Mrs. Bunche aboard the plane headed for Oslo and the December 10 ceremonies there. Ralph Johnson Bunche received the award before a notable audience that included the king and other members of Norway's royal family, diplomats and government officials, educators, and prominent men and women. After prolonged applause, Dr. Bunche made his brief acceptance speech in which, with deep feeling, he acknowledged his debt to the United Nations. He wished, he said, that he could share this "overwhelming honor" with those—especially Count Bernadotte—who gave their lives in Palestine in pursuit of peace.

In his Nobel lecture the following day, Ralph Bunche pleaded for education toward international living, for building moral as well as military strength, and for making spiritual as well as material progress. "Peace," he said, "cannot be achieved in a vacuum. Peace must be paced by human progress . . . translated into bread or rice, shelter, health and education, as well as freedom and human

dignity—a steadily better life." To these remarks he added,
"If the United Nations cannot ensure peace, there will be
none."

Dr. Bunche was made one of the two UN undersec-
retaries without department so that he might be on call for
diplomatic service anywhere in the world. As personal
troubleshooter for the second Secretary General, Dag
Hammarskjöld, Bunche directed UN peace-keeping activities in the Congo, Kashmir, and in the Middle East,
following the Suez Canal crisis.

Such devoted service wore down Ralph Bunche's athletic
body, and physical disabilities seriously affected his
eyesight and made walking difficult. Yet he continued to
work almost around the clock, negotiating, often behind the
scenes, and frequently flying halfway round the globe to
bring about better relations in some troubled area.

While working for worldwide harmony, Ralph Bunche
did not neglect the struggle for human rights being waged
by black Americans. In 1965, against doctor's orders, he
joined his friend Martin Luther King, Jr., in the Selma,
Alabama, freedom march, and three years later marched in
Dr. King's funeral procession. "By his own example," said
Roy Wilkins, head of the NAACP, "Ralph Bunche did as
much as anyone for the cause of the black man in
America."

Forced at last by his failing health to resign, Dr. Bunche
did so reluctantly, only two months before his death at
sixty-five. All around the world people paid tribute to this
"implacable worker in the cause of peace," the "heart,
brain, and right arm" of the United Nations. But no tribute
could have fitted him better than the one he himself had paid
to his friend and chief, Count Folke Bernadotte: "A zealot
for peace. Fearless. Indomitable. Indefatigable. A man of
unimpeachable integrity and boundless patience. A man
who, day after day, shook off adversity and frustration and
moved resolutely ahead, who pioneered in international
mediation, and who served the United Nations well."

Léon Jouhaux, the 1951 Nobel Peace Prize winner, was a Frenchman and a veteran leader of organized labor. Because of poverty he was forced to leave school and go to work when he was only twelve. He soon became active in

the local union of the match factory where he was employed. As a young man, he was an ardent revolutionary, although opposed to violence. He even tried, before the First World War, to organize French and German laborers in an anti-militaristic movement. When this failed, he supported his country in the war.

After World War I, Jouhaux tried to convert the working

class into a force for peace and social justice. He served as a French delegate to the Paris Peace Conference and later to the League of Nations. He pioneered in international labor legislation, drafting the charter for the International Labor Organization (ILO) and becoming a member of its administrative council. Conscious of his scanty schooling, Jouhaux continued his formal education, completing his studies while in his fifties. Following this, he wrote several books and a treatise on disarmament.

During the Second World War, Léon Jouhaux was imprisoned for several years in Nazi concentration camps. After his release, following the advance of the American army in Europe, he immediately resumed his activities as a labor leader. When he found that the Workers' Federation was infiltrated with Communists, he split with it and founded the Noncommunistic Workers Force. This he struggled to keep anti-communistic and nonmilitaristic. Jouhaux believed strongly in a United States of Europe and worked to promote it.

In receiving the Nobel Peace Prize, Léon Jouhaux said he felt the honor was not intended personally, but given as recognition of the value of the working class in the struggle for peace. In his eloquent Nobel address he declared: "There can be no peace as long as there is fear, need, distress, and injustice, but only when there is confidence and brotherhood." And he pleaded, "Let us be soldiers for peace."

1952

10. The Good Doctor of the Jungle

(Albert Schweitzer)

The 1952 Nobel Peace Prize, announced at the same time as the 1953 award, went to a person who had not been active in a peace organization, had not taken part in any peace negotiations between nations, and had not written or spoken primarily on peace. Yet men and women everywhere approved wholeheartedly the Nobel Committee's choice of **Albert Schweitzer,** medical missionary in French Equatorial Africa.

Dr. Schweitzer had prepared himself well for his greathearted service. Long before he earned the degree of doctor of medicine from the University of Strasbourg, Germany, he had become a doctor of philosophy, a doctor of theology, and a doctor of music. In each of these subjects his talent was considered outstanding.

Albert Schweitzer grew up in a small town of hilly, fertile Alsace, where his father was a minister. It was then a French province; in the war of 1870 it came under German rule, but the Alsatians never forgot the French language or customs. Albert was a sensitive boy—sensitive to nature, to music, and to the feelings of those around him. His interest in music, especially in organ music and most especially in the organ music of Bach, continued after he went to the University of Strasbourg. While earning degrees in philosophy and theology, he studied Bach with a famous Paris organist.

One morning during a vacation at home, the twenty-one-year-old Schweitzer awoke early. As he lay in bed, listening to the birds and thinking of his pleasant life at college and with his affectionate family, he began to wonder

what right he had to accept all his good fortune without doing something in return for those who were "wrestling with care and suffering." Solemnly he made a vow—he would go on gaining knowledge and living for himself until he was thirty; from then on he would devote himself "to the direct service of humanity."

Albert Schweitzer kept his decision to himself. He went back to the university and worked hard at his studies. He passed his first theological examination and won a scholarship to study philosophy at the Sorbonne in Paris. There he also studied again with the famous organist. Going to Berlin, he took a philosophy course, then returned to Strasbourg to receive his degree in philosophy. And then, like his father and grandfather, he became a preacher. Preaching, he wrote, "was a necessity of my being." A book grew out of his theological-degree thesis—*The Quest of the Historical Jesus*—and he also wrote an important book on the great composer for organ, Bach.

At thirty, Albert Schweitzer was well established as a minister, an author, a lecturer, and a musician. But the time he had given himself had run out and, according to his vow, he must now begin to devote himself to the service of humanity. He wanted to preach the gospel of love through work as well as words, to use his hands as well as his mind. From the Paris Missionary Society he learned of the need for doctors in the Congo. Being a doctor in Africa appealed to him, and he decided that this was what he would do, in spite of having to spend several years as a medical student to prepare for it.

Schweitzer's family and friends were appalled at his decision. They tried to dissuade him, but his mind was made up. He enrolled as a beginning student in the medical college of the University of Strasbourg, where he was now a professor of theology. He found the medical studies so demanding that he had to give up both his teaching and his preaching. For six long years Schweitzer fought his way through courses in anatomy and physiology, chemistry and bacteriology, medicine, surgery, and pharmacology, taking out a little time to practice on the organ and to give concerts to help with his school expenses.

At thirty-six, Schweitzer passed his medical examination, and a year later finished his term as a hospital intern and also a course in tropical medicine. Now at last he was ready for the life he had chosen; free, also, to marry. His bride, a professor's daughter, had taken a nursing course in order to help in the African hospital.By permission of the Paris Missionary Society, this hospital was to be established on the grounds of its mission at Lambaréné, French Equatorial Africa.

On Easter Day, 1913, Dr. and Mrs. Schweitzer set sail for West Africa—along with seventy boxes of equipment and medicines contributed by friends. Three weeks later they had crossed the equator and transferred to a paddle-wheel steamer that made its way up the great Ogowe River through green forests alive with monkeys. A dugout canoe took them the last stage of their journey. At the Lambaréné Mission, the Schweitzers were cordially welcomed and escorted to the little hilltop bungalow that was to be their home.

Early the next morning the patients began to arrive. They were suffering from sleeping sickness, malaria, heart trouble, dysentery, leprosy, and injuries from accidents and from wild animals. Dr. Schweitzer, with Mrs. Schweitzer's help, treated them in a whitewashed henhouse until the new building, made of corrugated iron, was ready. To the doctor, his patients were not cases but human beings in need. He would go out at night to check a pulse, speak comfortingly to the sleepless ones, or hold the hand of a feverish patient. "Black and white," he wrote, "sit side by side and feel that we know by experience the meaning of the words: 'And all ye are brethren.'"

The Paris Bach Society had presented Dr. Schweitzer with a piano built especially for the tropics; it was lined with zinc and had an organ pedal attachment. In the evenings he played on it, then attended to the endless correspondence—drugs and supplies to be ordered from Europe, letters to his family and to the friends who were making his work possible.

Gradually other hospital buildings followed the first, and the hillside began to look like a native village. Dr. Schweitzer knew the Africans would not come to a western-style hospital with stiff white beds and strange customs. Those who brought the sick often stayed to care for them and to cook over outdoor open fires. A few remained to become trusted helpers and interpreters.

When the First World War broke out, Dr. and Mrs. Schweitzer, being German citizens in a French colony, were interned as prisoners of war, but with permission to carry on the hospital work. Much disturbed by the war, Dr. Schweitzer took time to set down his thoughts in a journal. War, he reasoned, had come because man's spiritual progress had not kept pace with his material advances. The heart of the problem as he saw it lay in the phrase "reverence for life," and this ideal to him included all living things.

Later in the war the Schweitzers were deported from Lambaréné and shipped off to a prison camp in France. When their health was affected by the internment, they were exchanged for French prisoners and allowed to return to Alsace. After the armistice, Dr. Schweitzer worked in the Strasbourg city hospital and preached in a local church. He worried constantly about the African hospital and also about a large sum of money he had borrowed to help feed African natives in the early days of the war.

Suddenly an invitation to lecture in Uppsala, Sweden, came to him from Archbishop Söderblom—the man who, years before, had known Alfred Nobel in Paris and who was later, in 1930, to receive the Nobel Peace Prize. Dr. Schweitzer accepted the invitation, and in the brisk northern air and the congenial atmosphere of the archbishop's home he regained his health and confidence and energy. At

Archbishop Söderblom's suggestion, Dr. Schweitzer gave not only lectures but organ recitals and all over Sweden, as well as in Uppsala. In his lectures he used short, simple sentences, going over them with a capable interpreter and delivering them one or two at a time—a method he had used in giving Sunday talks at Lambaréné. His audiences seemed scarcely conscious that he was not speaking in Swedish. They were fascinated with his description of his African work, and to his delight donated enough money to pay off the debt that worried him and to begin a fund for future work.

Cheered by his success in Sweden, Dr. Schweitzer went on lecture tours in England and Switzerland and again in Sweden. In odd moments he wrote, and the income from his writings, lectures, and recitals built up the Lambaréné hospital fund. In February, 1924, Dr. Schweitzer headed again for Africa, taking with him an Oxford student. Mrs. Schweitzer remained in Europe as her health was not yet equal to life in the tropics; besides, there was now a small daughter.

Dr. Schweitzer found that the hospital had almost gone back to the jungles. He worked mornings as a doctor and afternoons as a carpenter, and slowly the old buildings were repaired. The increase in patients, however, clearly demanded a new hospital in wider spaces. Dr. Schweitzer chose a hilly spot a couple of miles up the river. With the help of volunteers, land was cleared from the jungle both for the hospital and for fruit orchards and vegetable gardens. From the corrugated-iron huts, built with hardwood framework and placed on piles, the natives could look down to their canoes in the river below.

Two doctors came from Europe, and two nurses. So did a motorboat contributed by friends in Sweden and another given by Danish friends. Now the doctors could travel to patients unable to come to the hospital. In January, 1927, the new hospital was opened, and Dr. Schweitzer wrote happily, "For the first time since I began to work in Africa my patients were housed as human beings should be."

With more doctors and nurses at the new Lambaréné hospital, Dr. Schweitzer was free to go to Europe to see his family and to earn needed money. In 1928 he received the Goethe Prize in Germany and used the money that accompanied it to build a house in the Alsace village of his childhood. This was to serve as the European headquarters of the Lambaréné hospital and also as a rest home for doctors and nurses on leave from there.

When Dr. Schweitzer returned to Africa in December, 1929, Mrs. Schweitzer went with him, leaving the daughter with relatives in Europe. By now the hospital had a well-equipped operating room and the drugs, all contributed by European and American friends, needed to deal with tropical diseases. Each year more and more doctors and nurses arrived, giving the doctor additional hours to devote to his writing and music and permitting him to return to Europe more frequently. His lectures, articles and books, and Bach recordings brought in money for growing hospital needs. Wherever he was, he took time to attend to his correspondence, doing most of the letter-writing himself, and in longhand.

In 1939, seeing the war clouds thickening, Dr. Schweitzer decided that his place was at his African hospital. Leaving his wife and daughter in Alsace, he returned to Lambaréné. The Second World War years were painful ones. Not only were the doctor's French and German friends fighting one another again, but his deepest feelings—his love of humanity, his devotion to peace and good will, his guiding principle of respect for life—were being violated by a world at war. To the natives' question, "Why are the whites, who brought us the gospel of love, now murdering each other?" he had no answer.

In 1940, the natives were terrified by air battles over Lambaréné. The hospital, which both the German and the Allied airmen were ordered not to bomb, became a refuge for both natives and whites. Luckily drugs and other essentials had reached Lambaréné before war actually broke out, and during the war the Albert Schweitzer Fellowship in America and organizations in Australia and New Zealand sent drugs and needed equipment. Even so, many patients had to be turned away.

In the midst of an unbroken nine-year stretch of duty, Albert Schweitzer celebrated his seventieth birthday—or rather others celebrated it while he worked as usual. Besides magazine articles, benefit concerts, and mention in sermons, there were radio broadcasts, one of which, originating in London, Dr. Schweitzer and his wife heard in Lambaréné.

Late in 1948, with the war over, the Schweitzers returned to Europe. Head silvery, powerful body weary from the long stay in the tropics and from overwork, "the good doctor" again gave lectures and organ recitals and continued to write down his thoughts on life and civiliza-tion. The next year, at seventy-four, he made his first trip to America, accompanied by his wife. At the Goethe Festival at Aspen, Colorado, Dr. Schweitzer lectured twice, once in French and once in German. So great was the rapport between him and his audience that the interpreter scarcely seemed needed. Dr. Schweitzer used the liberal fee to expand his leper colony and provide it with modern equipment and drugs.

By now the doctor's books had been translated into twenty languages, and many articles and books had been written about him. Wherever he went crowds came to see him and reporters to interview and photograph him. In 1951, he received the peace award of the West German Association of Book Publishers and Sellers, and also had the high honor of being elected to the French Academy.

Dr. Schweitzer was at Lambaréné in the fall of 1953 when the news of his being awarded the delayed 1952 Nobel Peace Prize came over the radio. "He put down his pen and covered his face with his hands, without saying a word," the assistant who heard the broadcast and brought him the news remembered. Later he said, "No man has the right to pretend that he has worked enough for the cause of peace or to declare himself satisfied."

Dr. Schweitzer's message to the Nobel Committee was read at the December 10 ceremony by the French ambassador to Norway. After expressing his appreciation of the honor, Dr. Schweitzer said he would use the prize money to replace the huts in the leper colony with permanent buildings. The next fall, with Mrs. Schweitzer, he journeyed to Oslo to deliver the Nobel address. Crowds jammed the streets to cheer "the greatest figure of our time." Students put on a torchlight procession, and the Norwegian king and queen received the distinguished guests at the palace. The Norwegian newspapers, through subscription, raised an amount even greater than the prize check, which also went to maintain the Lambaréné leper colony.

In his Nobel lecture, Dr. Schweitzer made an impassioned plea for people everywhere to rise above the thoughts of war and acquire the will to peace. "The spirit of the world," said the doctor, "is not directed toward peace." He quoted the words of the Apostle Paul: "If it be possible, so far as depends on you, live in peace with every man," and he added, "These words are not only for individuals but also for nations."

Within a few weeks Albert Schweitzer was back in Africa, supervising the construction of more buildings in the leper village and having the vegetable garden fenced in against wild animals. No longer operating, but still treating the natives' sicknesses skillfully and tenderly, the doctor daily added to his *Philosophy of Civilization* manuscript, practiced on his zinc-lined piano, chatted with his wife and associates, and played with the many pet animals that always surrounded him.

Almost every day brought visitors from distant places. Dr. Schweitzer talked with all of them, concerned himself about their comfort, and thanked them for coming. But it was they who had reason for thanks, for as one of them wrote: "In Lambaréné one finds peace and contentment; perfectness and concentrated energy; dedication to the simple and uncomplicated truth; love such as most of us dare not express, much less live. There is no consideration of race but simply of human beings, God's creatures. God is given his place in Lambaréné, and that perhaps explains the peacefulness of the day."

After his wife's death, the doctor stayed on in Lambaréné, continuing to work for the people of the jungle and also to try to set the world on the path to peace. He protested the testing of atomic weapons of mass destruction and warned that civilization would plunge to its doom unless men changed their ways and began to feel compassion for their fellowmen.

One morning, some months after his ninetieth birthday, Dr. Schweitzer toured the rambling hospital grounds in a jeep. Then, feeling tired, he lay down to rest. He fell into a coma from which he did not emerge. "He wanted to die as simply as possible," said his daughter, who was there.

Albert Schweitzer was buried beside his wife beneath the window of his room. Bells tolled; there was grief, but no sense of mourning. "You don't weep," one of his associates said, "when the leaves fall."

1953-1960
11. Reconstruction, Recovery, Reconciliation

(Marshall; Office of the United Nations High Commissioner for Refugees; Pearson; Pire; Noel-Baker; Luthuli)

No greater contrast can be imagined than that between Albert Schweitzer, winner of the 1952 Nobel Peace Prize, and **George Marshall,** the 1953 recipient. Yet, as one journalist remarked, each of these men "devoted his life, according to his lights, to the welfare of humanity."

George Marshall was the first professional soldier to be awarded the Nobel Peace Prize. Many questioned this prize being given to a man who had spent most of his life in the army. How, they asked, could a professional soldier ever be considered a true champion of peace? But the Nobel Committee had reasons for its choice.

After serving as the United States Chief of Staff during the Second World War, General George Marshall became the U.S. Secretary of State. It was while he was in this office that he proposed the plan that helped put a war-shattered Europe on its feet. The general first outlined his plan in a lecture delivered at Harvard University in 1947. It was that the United States should make a huge, long-term loan to the devastated western European countries. This aid program was authorized by the United States Congress. It came to be known as the Marshall Plan and it became one of the most important projects ever undertaken in an effort to promote peace. The vast amount of money poured into the war-torn countries worked as General

Marshall had foreseen, becoming largely responsible for Europe's economic recovery.

Like many military men, General Marshall had a real desire for peace. He was not only a gifted soldier, he was a man of great integrity with a lifelong devotion to the making of a better world.

The 1954 Nobel Peace Prize went to the **Office of the United Nations High Commissioner for Refugees,** the agency the UN had set up in Geneva after the Second World War to replace the expired International Office for

Refugees. Its organization and responsibilities were similar to those of that agency, directed by Fridtjof Nansen after the First World War. It was charged with resettling the refugees—between three and four hundred thousand of them—who were stranded after World War II in camps in Germany, Austria, Italy, and Greece. In addition, it was responsible for providing legal and social safeguards for the two million refugees who had already been resettled and were now scattered throughout the world.

Dr. G. J. van Neuven Goedhart, a Dutch editor and former Netherlands Minister of Justice, was the head, or high commissioner, of the new agency. He had been a leader in the resistance movement during the Second World War and then became chief of the Dutch delegation to the United Nations. Although the agency was hampered by inadequate funds, Dr. Goedhart and his staff did valiant and intelligent work. Among their worthwhile projects was the establishment throughout western Europe of vocational schools for refugees.

The Nobel Peace Prize was not awarded in 1955 or in 1956.

In 1957, the prize went for the first time to a Canadian. The winner, **Lester Pearson,** was an energetic, friendly person whom news reporters found they could rely on to give them frank and highly intelligent answers to their questions on international situations.

After being graduated from the University of Toronto, young Pearson entered a business office in Chicago, but left it when he won a fellowship at Oxford University in England. He specialized in history, then returned to Canada to teach the subject at his alma mater, coaching football on the side. Pearson's interest in history and international affairs led him naturally into the foreign service of his government. As first secretary of the foreign office, he attended conferences on disarmament and international law.

He was attached to the London office of Canada's high commissioner and served two years as Canadian ambassador to the United States.

In 1948, "Mike" Pearson entered his country's Parliament as a Liberal Party member. Immediately, Canada's voice in world affairs began to be more audible. Pearson was senior adviser to the Canadian delegation at the creation of the United Nations in San Francisco and for the next twelve years served as Canadian delegate to every UN General Assembly. He was chairman of the UN's Food and Agriculture Organization (FAO), of its Relief and Rehabilitation Administration (UNRRA), and of the General Assembly's fifty-five-member commission that created the special committee on Palestine. Its report formed the basis of the 1946 Palestine partition plan, and it was Delegate Pearson who drafted a plan for setting up the supervisory agency that helped preserve peace in the troubled area.

In the fall of 1952, Lester Pearson was elected president of the seventh session of the United Nations General Assembly. Impartial, taking the long view of things, and working to accomplish the UN aim "to maintain international peace and security," Pearson helped bring about a cease-fire in Korea and the creation of the North Atlantic Treaty Organization (NATO) as a collective "shield against aggression." He and Christian Lange of Norway and Gaetano Martino of Italy, jokingly referred to as the Three Wise Men, planned the reshaping and expansion of NATO's nonmilitary aspects.

Pearson's responsibility for Canada's foreign affairs did not diminish his concern over the uneasy peace based on the deterrent effects of nuclear weapons. He urged UN member nations neither to brandish arms about nor to discard them. Instead, he advocated the development of a bond stronger than one built on fear. He believed that trade would be one step in that direction, and to promote international trade, he went to Russia in 1958. He was the first foreign minister to go there since the Second World War. On his return,

Pearson stated his conviction that to avoid a perpetual state of tension, haunted by the fear of atomic war, we must "go forward toward genuine peace and cooperation between all peoples, forward to the solution of basic international issues which will bring about a feeling of security in the world."

Toward the end of 1956, Mr. Pearson played a large part in straightening out a conflict in the Middle East. After the United States and Great Britain withdrew their promise to finance the building of a dam on the Nile, Egypt's President Nasser retaliated by nationalizing the hitherto international Suez Canal. When negotiations broke down, troops from

Great Britain, France, and Israel advanced on Egypt. Egyptians blocked the Suez Canal, Syrians destroyed oil pipelines, and the Soviet Union came to the support of Egypt. Tensions mounted. Many even feared a third world war.

The United Nations, appealed to "to seek a settlement by peaceful means, and in conformity with the principles of justice and international law," voted to order the invading troops to withdraw. Then, by an overwhelming vote, it adopted Lester Pearson's suggestion that the UN create an international emergency force to maintain and supervise the cease-fire. In this way the world was pulled out of a crisis without a war and without violating the United Nations principles and charter. This UN action also prevented the collapse of the British Commonwealth of Nations and raised Canada to a key position among the world's nations. Looking to the future, the UN created a permanent Peace Supervisory Force. This was not an actual body, but a potential force to be made up of men and materials contributed by member nations when needed.

In 1957, Canada's Liberal Party, of which Lester Pearson had been Secretary of State for External Affairs for nine years, lost the election. Mr. Pearson retained his seat in the Canadian Parliament, but his days as head of Canada's foreign office and as Canadian representative to the United Nations, were over. The loss was a sad one, and not to Canada alone.

That same fall, Lester Pearson was informed that he had won the 1957 Nobel Peace Prize. He was, he said, "proud beyond words." He also remarked that he regarded the award as a tribute to Canada's efforts toward peace since the Second World War. A wire from UN Secretary General Hammarskjöld called the honor "a warmly deserved recognition of the consistently strong and intelligent support and leadership that through the years you have given to the cause of international peace."

Mr. Pearson called his Nobel lecture "The Four Faces of

Peace.'' These he listed as trade, power, diplomacy, and people. War conditions, he believed, were encouraged by inequalities; by lack of trade; by power—particularly power concentrated in two great world blocs facing each other in fear and hostility; by inflexible, unimaginative diplomacy; and by people. "We prepare for war like precocious giants and for peace like unimaginative pygmies.'' He pleaded for freer communication between peoples in order to bring about better relations and clear up misunderstandings "arising from ignorance [which] breeds fear—and fear remains the greatest enemy of peace.''

Soon after receiving the award, Mr. Pearson was elected head of Canada's Liberal Party, and in 1963 he became Canada's Prime Minister. National responsibilities did not lessen his interest in the international scene or his passion for peace. He served ably for five years; then the Conservative Party came into power, forcing him into private life.

In 1971, Lester Pearson died of cancer. He was mourned by all as, to quote his successor as prime minister, "a man of ability and good will [who] worked the better part of his life to make the world a better place for others.'' Pearson's statement that "peace is more than a word . . . it is something in the hearts of men'' will not be forgotten.

In 1958, the Nobel Peace Prize was awarded to a Belgian Dominican priest and social worker, **Dominique Georges Henri Pire.** Father Pire joined the Dominican order when he was eighteen. After receiving his training in Rome and at the University of Louvaine, he returned to his home town of Huy to teach moral philosophy and sociology at its monastery.

In World War II, Father Pire worked as chaplain and intelligence officer in the underground resistance movement. Even before the end of the war, he began to carry out some of his imaginative plans to help the underprivileged. One project was to find "godparents" who would send

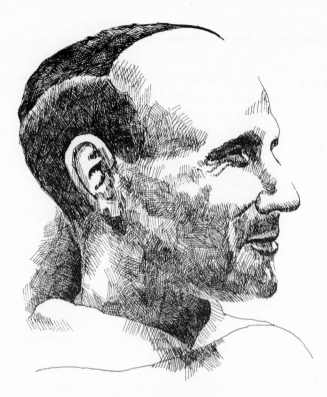

needy children gifts, letters, and food, and sometimes finance country vacations for city girls and boys. After the war, Father Pire enlarged his work to include camps for displaced persons and homes for the elderly, ill, and handicapped who were not permitted to emigrate to other countries.

The compassionate priest's most ambitious undertaking was the establishment of several small communities where refugees could begin to become self-dependent and find their way back into normal life. Calling this undertaking "Aid to Displaced Persons," he set up "villages" in various European countries with headquarters in Huy, Belgium, where he continued to teach at the monastery.

Father Pire was forty-eight when he won the award—much younger than most Nobel Peace Prize winners. He was tall, broad-shouldered, and strong, with a contagious sense of humor and an engaging smile. Someone remarked that, standing in his white Dominican robe among the black-coated figures at the award ceremony, he looked "like a candle on a dark altar."

The $41,420 check that accompanied Father Pire's medal and certificate would, he said, be used for his humanitarian work—feeding the hungry, building more homes for the homeless, and creating additional "villages" to bring security and self-sufficiency to displaced persons.

A seventy-year-old British statesman, **Philip John Noel-Baker,** received the 1959 Nobel Peace Prize. Born a Quaker, Noel-Baker spent much of his life in the effort to promote peace, especially through disarmament. He was educated at the American Friends college at Haverford, Pennsylvania, and at Cambridge University, England. In the First World War, he served at the front with an ambulance corps; afterward, he became Lord Robert Cecil's secretary, first at the Paris Peace Conference and later at the League of Nations in Geneva. There he also worked in the Secretariat and attended the Assembly as a member of the British delegation. In 1924, he returned to England to become a professor of international relations at the University of London.

Elected to Parliament as a member of the Labor Party, Noel-Baker held several important posts in the cabinet during the Labor Party's days of power. He attended the 1932–1933 Geneva Disarmament Conference as assistant to Arthur Henderson. Not only was Noel-Baker connected with the League of Nations, he helped draft the charter of the United Nations, was present when it was created at San Francisco in 1945, and attended its first General Assembly.

In a book entitled *The Arms Race: A Programme for World Disarmament,* Noel-Baker warned against the widespread apathy of men and women because they "have not grasped what the modern armaments mean. . . . Armaments produce fear, and fear produces more armaments."

When Philip Noel-Baker received the Nobel Peace Prize, it was commented that he amply fulfilled the requirement in Nobel's will that the award should go to the man or woman "who had done the most or best work to further brotherhood among the peoples, to abolish or cut down standing armies, to create or further the work of peace conferences."

Announcement of the 1960 Nobel Peace Prize was made simultaneously with that of the 1961 award. According to the press, the delay was caused by the difficulty the Nobel Committee had in making "its exhaustive search into the qualifications" of the 1960 candidate, **Albert John Luthuli.** With the Committee's announcement of the 1960 winner, much interest was shown in the fact that Luthuli was a Zulu chieftain and the African leader of the resistance movement against the Union of South Africa. He was, it was learned, confined to his native village by the South

African government because of his acts of defiance against its policy of racial segregation and discrimination.

White liberals of South Africa, including the novelist Alan Paton, hailed the Nobel Committee's choice of Chief Luthuli. The government of South Africa, however, called the selection "irresponsible" and an unfriendly gesture against the Union of South Africa.

The newsman who told Chief Luthuli of the honor said the chief was "stunned" and insisted on spending several hours alone before being interviewed. Then, acknowledging that the award would bring him both "spiritual encouragement" and "added responsibility," he said he accepted it only as a representative of his fellow Africans and those others who had worked for better race relations in South Africa. When told that the South African government claimed that he was a dangerous extremist, anti-white, and a Communist, Luthuli denied the charges. He was, he said, a moderate and something of a socialist of the British variety; he was not anti-white, only anti-white supremacist; and he had no desire to dominate, only to share.

Albert Luthuli had spent his early boyhood in the home of his uncle, the Zulu chieftain of the village of Groutville in the province of Natal. He then lived with an older brother in his mother's nearby hut, and from there left to attend a mission boarding school. When far enough advanced, he took the teacher-training course the school offered. Because of his good work, he was selected to take the higher teachers' training course at Adams College, also in Natal. There he remained for fifteen years, first as a student, then as a teacher.

Early in his school life, Luthuli showed a talent for organization. He served as secretary, then president of the African Teachers' Association. He also helped found the Zulu Language and Cultural Society with the idea of preserving the best in the Zulu heritage and adding to it values from the European culture. Visitors who came to Adams College broadened Luthuli's education and outlook.

He married Nokukhanya, a student teacher. He spent holidays and vacations at the home they made in Groutville, near his aging mother, while continuing to teach at Adams.

Luthuli gave up his teaching, which he enjoyed, when the five thousand people of Groutville elected him to be their chief. He found satisfaction in administering the small town, and he took special pleasure in the court sessions where, assisted by the tribal elders, he settled disputes and disagreements. He called this part of his work "thrashing things out in the attempt to get at the truth." As chief, Luthuli made numerous reforms, among them admitting women to the tribal councils, closing the beer halls run by whites for the use of Africans, and organizing the sugarcane growers of the region—sugarcane being Natal's chief industry.

One of the great problems of the Zulu people was the

small amount and poor quality of the land on which they had to depend for a living. The government allotted only 13 percent of the land to Africans, although they made up 70 percent of the people. In addition, the best land was retained for white farmers; Africans were expected to get along with the rest, and without badly needed fertilizer or agricultural machines.

Political meetings gave Chief Luthuli the opportunity to travel to Durban, the capital of Natal, and to other cities. He learned much from his encounters with different kinds of people, including educated men and women of other races—white, Asian, and "coloured" (those of mixed blood). He became a member of the Durban Joint Council of Europeans and Africans and of the Institute of Race Relations. He also served as an executive on the interracial Christian Council of South Africa, and in 1938 was its delegate to an international missionary conference in India. This experience brought Luthuli into contact with Christian leaders from all over the world and gave him, as he wrote, "a sense of the vigor of Christianity" and "wider sympathies and wider horizons."

In 1948, after the Second World War, Chief Luthuli was invited to the United States to speak to young people in summer camps and at gatherings in several large cities. On southern campuses he met and talked with many black Americans, and in the cities he encountered some racial segregation. The nine-month American tour, he said, enabled him to "see South African issues more sharply and in a different and larger perspective."

The South African government had passed in 1910, an Act of Union that defined African, Indian, and "coloured people" as "subject races." Two years later, in response to this, the "subject races" formed the African National Congress. Its objectives were "to fight the total exclusion of the African from the management of South Africa, to give direction to the forces of liberation, to harness peacefully the growing resistance to continued oppression and, by various nonviolent means, to demand the redress of injustice.''

For years the organization made little headway, but when the government declared it would never permit nonwhites to become fellow citizens, tension mounted. Increased oppression brought on increased resistance and the African National Congress became more active. It took a stand against the oppressive Land Acts and against the law compelling nonwhites to carry passes—a system that Chief Luthuli said was an effort ''to control the whole life of all Africans'' and to make them ''landless pawns.''

In 1949, when the African National Congress started a defensive campaign called a Programme of Action, Chief Luthuli helped promote its plans for demonstrations, protest strikes, and other nonviolent acts of disobedience. In 1952, after being elected A.N.C.'s president, Luthuli did not mince his words. The land, he declared, did not belong to the whites; Africans had a right ''to walk freely in our own land.''

The South African government, alarmed by Luthuli's free speech and disturbing activities, took his chieftainship away from him. His tribesmen, however, continued to regard him as their chief and refused to select a successor. The government's policy of bannings and banishments included an order forbidding Luthuli to enter cities or to attend any public gatherings. The following year he was forbidden to travel more than thirty miles from his Groutville home.

Stress and strain gave Chief Luthuli, who already suffered from high blood pressure, a slight stroke. In order to have him moved to a Durban hospital, his wife had to receive permission from government officials. After a two-month hospital stay, the chief returned to Groutville and immediately plunged into work. The Freedom Charter he helped prepare, spelling out the relief Africans sought from oppression, was adopted at a Congress of the People called by the African National Congress.

The South African government, realizing that the resistance movement was in dead earnest, took drastic action; it arrested more than eight thousand nonwhites. Police appeared at Chief Luthuli's home in the middle of the night, charged him with high treason, and took him to Durban. From there, he was flown with other Africans to Johannesburg, where he was arraigned and jailed. The jail was soon overflowing with prisoners. They came, said Luthuli, "from every corner of the land—professionals and laborers, priests and lawyers, Muslims, Christians, Hindus, infidels, Africans, Indians, Coloureds." Europeans too, for resistance had become more than a matter of color. "More significant than the colour bar," wrote Chief Luthuli, "is the bar which stands between those who place their faith in rule by force and violence, and those who repudiate the police state."

True to his nature, Chief Luthuli at once began to turn the prison experience to good account. Ironically, he noted, the government had provided in jail what it had previously denied to Africans—a meeting place and time for discussion.

The 1956 high-treason trials went on for many weeks, some of which Luthuli had to spend in a hospital, downed again by dangerously high blood pressure. Finally, the government abandoned the trials and released Chief Luthuli along with many others. Three years later, it placed him under another ban, this time for publicly burning his detested pass and encouraging others to do the same. The new ban was to last five years. During this time he was forbidden to take part in any political activity, to receive visitors, or to leave Groutville.

It was in his enforced retreat in October, 1962, that Chief Luthuli received the news that he had won the Nobel Peace Prize. At first it was doubtful that he would be allowed to go to Oslo to accept the award, but the South African government grudgingly issued a ten-day pass, and a few weeks later Luthuli and his faithful wife, Nokukhanya, boarded a plane for Norway.

In wintry Oslo, friends wrapped the chief and his wife in unaccustomed furs, though Chief Luthuli said, "I do not feel the cold because I am meeting so many warmhearted people." And he added, "How great is the paradox and how much greater the honor that an award in support of peace and the brotherhood of man should come to one who is a citizen of a country where the brotherhood of man is an illegal doctrine."

At the formal ceremony on December 10 in the great hall of the University of Oslo, Albert John Luthuli appeared in the ceremonial costume of a tribal chieftain, with flowing blue and black robe, leopard-skin cap, and leopard-teeth necklace. In his Nobel address the following day, the chief spoke "for all that is best in South Africa." The struggle going on there, he said, was "not for wealth or land or domination, but for the recognition and preservation of the rights of man and the establishment of a truly free world for a free people." And he predicted: "In a strife-torn world, tottering on the brink of complete destruction by man-made nuclear weapons, a free and independent Africa is in the making." All were impressed by the black leader's words and by his innate dignity, combined with deep humility.

Chief Luthuli went back to his restricted life on his small Natal farm. Forbidden as he was to engage in political activity, the nonviolent chief was replaced by impatient younger black agitators who, to his dismay, employed sabotage and violence in the attempt to gain their ends.

In 1967, Chief Luthuli's life came to an abrupt and tragic end. Now deaf and partly blind, he was struck by a train and fatally injured when crossing the track in Groutville. Yet, although at times the black extremists seemed to have taken over the movement to achieve a nonracist society in South Africa, it was certain that Chief Luthuli's principles of moderation and nonviolence would never be entirely forgotten.

1961-1963
12. Crosscurrents in the Atomic Age

(Hammarskjöld; Pauling; International Committee of the Red Cross and League of Red Cross Societies)

According to the Nobel Committee regulations, if a person who had been nominated for the Nobel Peace Prize died after the nominations were closed and before the date of the next award, he or she could be given the prize posthumously. **Dag Hammarsjköld,** one of the nominees for the 1961 Nobel Peace Prize, was killed in a plane crash in Africa in September, 1961. A month later, the Nobel Committee announced that the 1961 Nobel Peace Prize had been awarded to him posthumously.

Dag Hammarskjöld was the Secretary General of the United Nations. He had followed the Norwegian, Trygve Lie, who served as the first UN Secretary General. No one could have been better prepared than Hammarskjöld to head this organization created "to maintain international peace and security." Dag was the youngest of four sons of a highly respected top official in the Swedish government. After being graduated from the University of Uppsala, he studied in the fields of law, finance, and economics, and then entered government service. He wrote later that he had inherited from a long line of government officials the belief that "no life was more satisfactory than one of selfless service to your country—or humanity."

Beginning as a secretary, young Hammarskjöld rose quickly to an administrative position in the unemployment commission. During the depression years, he had a chance to try out many of his economic ideas. In World War II, Hammarskjöld was sent by neutral Sweden to England to negotiate financial matters with the Norwegian government in exile there. After the war, as a member of the Executive Committee for European Economic Cooperation, he helped activate the Marshall Plan for European reconstruction. His economic expertise, his gift for languages, and his knack for "finding formulas of agreement" made his service of real value. In addition, from his four months on the Continent he gained essential training in international affairs. This experience led to his becoming Sweden's Minister of Foreign Affairs.

It was a difficult time, with mounting international tensions and increasing disagreements between western nations and the Soviet Union. Nowhere were these disagreements felt more keenly than in the young United Nations. To fill the post of Secretary General in 1953, it was important to find a man of integrity who was a skilled diplomat, devoted to the cause of peace, and unquestionably loyal to the United Nations. Dag Hammarskjöld was such a man, and he was invited to become the UN's second Secretary General.

Upon accepting the "overwhelming job," Hammarskjöld expressed his belief that "the private man should disappear and the international public servant take his place." From the start he asserted the authority given him by the United Nations Charter and, always working within it, became the UN's effective guide and leader.

Hammarskjöld's first job was to establish a harmonious atmosphere within the Secretariat and make it an efficient working body. To do this, he set up a sort of international civil service, requiring employees to replace national attitudes with complete loyalty to the United Nations.

Always a hard worker, Hammarskjöld often stayed in his nineteenth-floor office until late at night—sometimes even until dawn. Letters, wires, and cables in many languages poured in, especially when some important matter was under consideration in the General Assembly or Security

Council. It was fortunate that the Secretary General read quickly and understandingly in several languages.

The first specific assignment handed Mr. Hammarskjöld by the General Assembly was to try to secure the release of eleven American airmen being held prisoner by the Chinese. Although the Red China government was pretty much sealed off, Hammarskjöld was received in Peking by Premier Chou En-lai, with whom he had several lengthy conversations. After a face-saving interval, the airmen were released. Hammerskjöld had survived his first diplomatic test.

Next came the attempt to keep the Arab-Israeli hostility from erupting into open warfare. By gaining the confidence of both sides and establishing his "personal ascendancy" over the situation, Hammerskjöld was able to avert war. In 1956, during the Suez crisis, when Britain, France, and Israel combined to force Egypt to relinquish the Suez Canal, which it had taken over, Secretary General Hammarskjöld worked almost endlessly. After the UN achieved a cease-fire, he insisted that it follow Lester Pearson's recommendation and use the newly created United Nations Peace Supervisory Force, the world's first truly international military body, to police the area. This action resulted in a resounding victory for the United Nations. Again, when disorders in Lebanon and Jordan brought British and American troops to the scene, Hammarskjöld, using the UN Charter as authority, managed their withdrawal.

In 1957, in the midst of the growing intensity of the Cold War, Dag Hammarskjöld was unanimously appointed to a second four-year term. But the big powers were increasingly bypassing the United Nations, and their attitudes toward it "blew hot and cold depending on how their interests were affected." While observing strict neutrality, Hammarskjöld tried to persuade the member nations to make more use of the United Nations. He encouraged cooperative projects and was largely responsible for two international scientific conferences on the peaceful use of atomic energy; these resulted in a sharing of nuclear-power knowledge.

The character of the United Nations was changing with the inclusion of many small nations. From four African member nations in 1953, when Hammarskjöld came to the UN, the number grew to twenty-six in 1960 and continued to increase. The Secretary General found need for all his diplomatic skills. There was also the necessity for more frequent journeys to try to achieve "peace by prevention." Hammarskjöld kept a packed suitcase in his office, ready for immediate take-off. Seldom did he find time to relax or spend weekends in his country retreat a few miles north of the city.

Hammarskjöld made several trips to Africa to acquaint himself firsthand with its problems and personalities. In 1960, a political explosion in the Congo brought a request for the United Nation troops, and Dag Hammarskjöld saw to the assembling of a force of thirty-five hundred men, largely

African. At first, everything went fairly smoothly. Then, because of personal ambitions and tribal differences, the situation deteriorated rapidly. Hammarskjöld stood firm, insisting on a neutral, conciliatory policy and refusing to allow the UN troops to be used for personal advantage.

The hostile attitude of the Russian leader, Nikita Khrushchev, added to the Secretary General's difficulties. Khrushchev came to the United Nations, denounced Mr. Hammarskjöld, and vociferously demanded the replacement of his office by a three-man Secretary Generalship, which, he said, would more fairly represent the socialist states. Mr. Hammarskjöld, in quietly replying to Mr. Khrushchev's tirade, pointed out that both the United Nations Charter and the good of the organization called for a single, strong administrator. As to his personal decision, he stated: "It is very easy to resign; it is not so easy to stay on. . . . I shall remain at my post during the term of my office as a servant of the organization."

The tumultuous applause that greeted Dag Hammarskjöld's words left no doubt that when his term expired, he would be reelected. The battering of the Communist bloc, however, made it difficult for the Secretary General to work effectively. He responded to the Soviet's mounting demand that he delegate more of his authority by increasing Secretariat personnel and making other changes designed to make it more efficient.

In May, 1961, on the occasion of receiving an honorary degree at Oxford University, Mr.Hammarskjöld delivered a lengthy lecture on the subject of the international servant. Challenging Mr. Khrushchev's statement that "no man can be neutral," he upheld the concept of an "independent, international civil service" and of a United Nations headed by a Secretary General whose tasks "involved the exercise of political judgment."

September 8, 1961, was Staff Day at the United Nations. Before setting out for Africa on a mission of peace, the Secretary General addressed the Secretariat staff. He told

them that the member governments would soon decide
whether the Secretariat would exist merely as a provider of
necessary administrative services or as the truly international body envisioned in the United Nations Charter. If the
latter, he said, it then "may develop as an instrument for the
preservation of peace and security of increasing significance
and responsibilities." He urged his staff "to maintain their
professional pride, their sense of purpose, and their
confidence in the higher destiny of the organization itself,
by keeping to the highest standards of personal integrity in
their conduct as international civil servants and in the
quality of their work." They could, he said, take pride in
the organization's accomplishments. "Let us work in the
conviction that our work has meaning beyond the
narrow individual one and has meant something for man."
It was his last speech.

All around the world the news that Dag Hammarskjöld
had been killed in a plane crash while on a peace mission in
Africa brought shock and sadness. Few men have had such
tribute paid to them. In his native Sweden, thousands of
mourners marched in a torchlight procession, while all over
the country bells tolled. Notables from many countries came
to attend his near-royal funeral in the Uppsala Cathedral,
and in England a memorial service was held in Westminster
Abbey to honor "a faithful servant of humanity."

The American press recalled the late United Nations
Secretary General's twenty "missions for peace" and
quoted his words: "The work for peace must be animated
by tolerance and the work for human rights by respect for
the individual." *Newsweek* commented: "In his actions the
United Nations wielded power; in his courage the United
Nations staved off threats; in his vision the United Nations
developed a purpose and a personality."

At the United Nations memorial service for its lost
Secretary General, Beethoven's Ninth Symphony was
rebroadcast from the United Nations Day concert the
previous year, along with the brief introductory remarks the

Secretary General had made on that occasion. In them he had compared Beethoven's "final hymn of praise" with the United Nations Charter, which also, he had said, led from "conflict and emotion to reconciliation" and "reaffirmed faith in the dignity and worth of the human person."

Linus Pauling, distinguished idealistic scientist, received the 1962 Nobel Peace Prize. In 1954, he had received the Nobel Prize in chemistry. In the Nobel Foundation's more than half-century of existence, this was the first time anyone had received two Nobel prizes.

Before he was thirty, many had noted the scientific talent of Linus Pauling, a native of the state of Washington and a resident of California, and his fame had spread beyond the West Coast and even beyond America. Pauling's bent toward science had begun early. In high school, because he neglected all subjects except scientific ones, the school authorities refused him his diploma. This did not daunt young Pauling. He went on to Oregon State College, where he majored in chemical engineering. Then he studied for an advanced degree at the California Institute of Technology, popularly known as Cal Tech; and because of his outstanding ability, he was made a teaching fellow.

Armed with his Ph.D. *summa cum laude,* a grant from Cal Tech, a National Research Fellowship, a Guggenheim Fellowship, and an Oregon bride, Linus Pauling traveled to Europe for further study. Leaders in the field of advanced chemistry welcomed him to work with them in research into crystal and molecular structure and a new theory of quantum mechanics.

Dr. and Mrs. Pauling returned to California after two years abroad, and he became a professor at Cal Tech. Within a short time, he published many important papers; and from the American Chemical Society, he received its award given to "young chemists of great promise."

At forty, Dr. Pauling was called "the outstanding theoretical chemist of the United States and probably of the

world.'' He now directed the Gates and Crellin Laboratories at Cal Tech, and from them flowed scientific papers and books that brought renown to him and his staff. European students traveled to California to work under Dr. Pauling, and he went to Europe frequently to attend and speak at international scientific gatherings.

In the Second World War, Dr. Pauling contributed his scientific skill to the United States government. Among other things, he developed rocket explosives for the Navy. For his services, he was awarded the Presidential Medal for Merit. Resuming his teaching and research at Cal Tech, Dr. Pauling used a new and unusual approach for investigating the structure of organic proteins: the interrelation of different branches of science (chemistry, physics, and biology) in the effort to develop drugs that could combat disease.

The coming of the atomic age changed Dr. Pauling's goal. Like many other scientists, he had been disturbed by the dropping of atomic bombs on Hiroshima and Nagasaki. Albert Einstein, acknowledged scientific world leader, and seven other eminent scientists formed the Emergency Committee of Atomic Scientists. Their purpose was to warn the world of the dangers of nuclear power and the absolute necessity of substituting reason for war. Linus Pauling joined them with enthusiasm.

To the scientists' dismay, the American people were reluctant to face the fact that there was no defense against the atomic bomb. Instead, they were proud that the United States possessed the ultimate weapon of war. Most of the Emergency Committee, disillusioned by resistance to their scientific arguments, gave up their mission and returned to their laboratories. Dr. Pauling, however, went on crusading against the manufacture, stockpiling, spread, and use of nuclear weapons. Because he believed so completely in the necessity for peace, he supported "nearly every peace movement that came to my attention." This got him into trouble, as did his connections with scientists in Communist countries. He was vice-president of the World Federation of Scientific Workers, and his association with its communistic president, Joliot-Curie, was questioned.

In 1952, the Royal Society of London honored Dr. Pauling by inviting him to address its members on one of his important new scientific discoveries. To his embarrassment, he had to decline the invitation because the U.S. Department of State refused to renew his passport. Although Dr. Pauling had stated under oath that he was not and never had been a Communist or a Communist sympathizer, the State Department claimed that the journey "was not in the best interests of the United States." Pauling was also denied clearance to go to other countries, including India, where he had been invited to speak at the dedication of a new laboratory. More than the personal humiliation, Dr. Pauling lamented the opportunity the United States was missing to "take the lead in bringing sanity into the world, abolishing the terrifying threat of a hydrogen-bomb war and the destruction of civilization, and initiating a future of worldwide law and order." He was questioned as to his membership in peace organizations, and he insisted that he had a right to support any movement that seemed to him to "increase the chance for a peaceful future."

But when Dr. Pauling was notified in 1954 that he had been awarded the Nobel Prize in chemistry, the Department of State provided him with a passport that would enable him to go to Stockholm, where the scientific and literary Nobel prizes were awarded, and also to any other country he wished to visit. The government was perhaps beginning to realize the truth of the scientists' assertions that its restrictive passport policy, by denying free exchange of ideas, was hampering scientific advances.

As nuclear testing by both the United States and the Soviet Union increased, Dr. Pauling carried on a vigorous campaign to warn the public of the dangers of radiation. A petition he prepared, urging an international agreement to stop the nuclear testing, was signed by eleven thousand persons in fifty countries. It was presented to the United Nations, and when nothing came of it there, Dr. Pauling published a book, *No More War!* in which he told the story of the petition and repeated his warnings.

A Senate Internal Security subcommittee, interested in learning whether Communists were involved in the test-ban petition, asked Dr. Pauling to name those who had helped collect the signatures. This Dr. Pauling refused to do, for fear, he said, of bringing reprisals on "idealistic, high-minded workers for peace." The time-consuming congressional inquiry came to nothing, and Linus Pauling went back to his laboratories. He also continued his lecturing crusade for peace, influencing many, especially young people, to work for disarmament. On his occasional trips to foreign countries, Dr. Pauling met more and more people concerned about nuclear arms and eager to bring about peace.

Over the years, many awards and honorary degrees came

to Linus Pauling. When he was notified that he had the distinction of winning his second Nobel Prize, he said that the Nobel Peace Prize meant even more to him than the Nobel Prize in chemistry "because I feel so strongly about the need for peace and an end to human suffering from wars." As had happened several times before, the announcement of the award was delayed for several months; and although the honor was for 1962, the actual awarding of the prize was made on December 10, 1963.

At that ceremony, Gunnar Jahn, chairman of the Nobel Committee, spoke of Linus Pauling's campaign against the testing, spread, and use of nuclear weapons and "against all warfare as a means of solving international conflicts." In his Nobel address, which he called "Science and Peace," Dr. Pauling credited scientific discoveries with forcing the world into "a period of peace and reason." He hoped the United Nations would take over the supervision of nuclear stockpiles and he predicted that "the great goal of a world without war is in sight."

After many years with the California Institute of Technology, Dr. Pauling left it to join a new organization, the Center for the Study of Democratic Institutions. This organization had been established to investigate "the impact of science, technology, and war on democratic societies," and Dr. Pauling felt that within it he could better promote disarmament and peace. He continued his independent research in experimental medicine and his extensive lecturing against war. Repeatedly he warned, "No dispute between nations can justify nuclear war," and he expressed optimism that someday the world's resources and the discoveries of science would be used "for the benefit of all human beings all over the world and to develop a culture worthy of man's intelligence."

In 1975, President Ford presented to Dr. Pauling the prestigious National Medal of Science, citing him for "the extraordinary scope and power of his imagination" during his "long and distinguished career."

In 1963, the Nobel Peace Prize, announced simultaneously with the 1962 award to Dr. Pauling, went to the **International Committee of the Red Cross** and the **League of Red Cross Societies.** The twenty-five members of the International Committee were all Swiss citizens who served without pay. The League was made up of the national Red Cross societies in different countries—more than a hundred of them, with a membership of close to two million. The League was not under the control of the International Committee, but worked closely with it.

Twice before—in 1917, at the close of the First World War, and in 1944, at the end of World War II—the Red Cross had been honored by the Nobel Peace Prize Committee. On the first occasion, the Committee had recognized a Red Cross that had handled communication with prisoners of war and inspection of their camps, the exchange of wounded soldiers, and aid to interned aliens. The second time, the award honored a Red Cross whose volume of war work was much greater, more varied, and of even greater significance. Now, in the hundredth year of the organization's existence, and in a year of comparative peace, the award of the Nobel Peace Prize could be interpreted as recognizing not only the Red Cross wartime accomplishments, but also its service in time of peace. Citizens everywhere, struck by natural disasters such as floods, tornadoes, tidal waves, fires, or other catastrophes, could testify to the compassionate, effective work of the Red Cross. It was good that once again the Red Cross motto, "Not for glory but for service," be brought to the attention of the world.

At the 1963 ceremonies in Oslo, D. Max Huber, acting president of the International Committee, spoke of the ideals kept alive by the Red Cross through a difficult century. They were, he said, ideals of human decency, humanity, and hope—ideals that are "the preliminary condition for any community of man."

1964
13. Nonviolent Crusader for Social Justice

(Martin Luther King, Jr.)

The five members of the Nobel Peace Prize Committee did not always agree on the man or woman to receive what is probably the world's most highly regarded honor. In 1964, however, the Committee voted unanimously to award the Nobel Peace Prize to **Martin Luther King, Jr.,** black leader of the struggle for racial justice in America.

Few needed to ask, Who is this man? for the name of Martin Luther King, Jr., had been continually headlined in the American press since 1956. At that time Dr. King had gained prominence as the leader of a Negro bus boycott in Montgomery, Alabama. Since then, his persistent, nonviolent campaigning for long-denied rights for blacks had won a large following among both black and white Americans.

As the son of the pastor of the Ebenezer Baptist Church in Atlanta, Georgia, Martin grew up in a pleasant black district of that city. He played with the neighborhood children, attended the all-black neighborhood school, and at fifteen entered Morehouse College, a private institution for black male students. His rather domineering father wanted his son to become a minister, but it was not until his senior year that Martin decided on the ministry as his lifework.

After graduation from Morehouse College, he entered Crozier Theological Seminary in Pennsylvania. Here Martin became exposed to life in an integrated institution in a northern, white-dominated society. He found his new environment stimulating and quickly made friends among both black and white students. His capacity for leadership was evidenced by his being elected president of the student government.

In 1951, young King received his degree of Bachelor of Divinity. But instead of carrying out his father's desire that he become assistant pastor of the Ebenezer Baptist Church, Martin showed his independence by entering Boston University to work for his Ph.D. While making progress in his studies, he found time to make new friends, one of whom was Coretta Scott, a voice student at the New England Conservatory of Music. Before long, Martin told Coretta, "You have all of the qualities that I expect to find in the girl I'd like to have for a wife."

Coretta and Martin were married in 1953. After they completed their studies in Boston, Dr. King became the pastor of the Dexter Avenue Baptist Church in Montgomery, Alabama.

Bus-riding had long been a humiliating experience for the black people of Montgomery. After paying their fare at the front of the bus, they had to get off and reenter at the back to sit in the black-only rear section. One day in December, 1955, a very tired black woman, Mrs. Rosa Parks, refused to give up her seat to a white person and remained seated in spite of a great uproar. This rebellious act inspired a bus boycott among the Negroes. At a mass meeting, black bus-riders and sympathizers agreed to organize car pools to go to work, or to walk if necessary. They chose young Dr. King as the leader of the bus boycott movement. Influenced by the examples of Jesus, Gandhi, and Thoreau, he called for a campaign of passive resistance.

The month after the boycott started, Dr. King's home was bombed. Fortunately, his wife and baby and a lady caller, who were inside the house, were unharmed. Dr. King dissuaded the black friends gathered in front of his house from violent retaliation. Two days later, however, several black citizens of Montgomery filed suit against the bus company and the city. In retaliation, more than a hundred black men and women, including Dr. King, were arrested

and charged by the Montgomery County grand jury with having conspired to destroy a legitimate business—the bus company.

Instead of stopping the bus boycott, the mass arrests strengthened it. Americans all over the country became interested in the confrontation. Top reporters came to Montgomery, wanting pictures and stories about the protest movement and its leader. The *New York Times* described Dr. King as "a rather soft-spoken man with a bearing and maturity beyond his twenty-seven years," and wrote at length about his southern upbringing and northern education. One writer commented, "Circumstances and history, opposition and support have combined to make him known around the world."

When the judge pronounced Dr. King guilty at his trial in March, 1956, there was an uproar among his followers. They promised that whatever happened, they would continue with their nonviolent resistance. The verdict was immediately appealed, though the court battle went on for a little more than a year. Then bus segregation was declared unconstitutional by the United States Supreme Court, and on December 21, 1956, integrated buses began to run in Montgomery.

By this time, the black civil-rights movement had become nationwide. Dr. King was a man "on the go," carrying his message of nonviolent resistance to injustice to large audiences all over the country. His dramatic appeals were having an enormous effect and were bringing on him both extravagant praise and bitter attacks. He was called a "courageous fighter for equal civil rights," a "contender of justice for all peoples," a "fearless foe of injustice and inhumanity," and an "uncompromising champion of enduring principles." At the same time, he was accused of racial agitation, of self-exploitation, of building a fortune for himself, and of being a Communist.

To take a well-earned rest, Dr. and Mrs. King flew to Africa to attend the ceremonies marking the birth of a new nation, Ghana. It was an unforgettable experience for them; they found it inspiring to meet internationally illustrious men and women. Later, they found equally inspiring the pilgrimage they made to India, where they met Nehru and paid homage at Gandhi's shrine.

A conference of southern black leaders, mostly ministers, set up the organization that became the Southern Christian Leadership Conference. One of its first acts was a "Prayer Pilgrimage for Freedom to Washington in 1957. A great crowd, 90 percent black, gathered before the Lincoln Memorial to listen to Dr. King's stirring speech in which he pleaded, "Give us the ballot!"

As the cry of the black population for political action grew louder, popular sentiment forced Congress to pass the first civil-rights legislation in more than eighty years. Dr. King and other black leaders were invited to meet with President Eisenhower in the White House. According to nationwide publicity they considered together the need for a program of education, for passing a stronger civil-rights bill, and for the more vigorous enforcement of existing laws.

One morning when Dr. King appeared at court in Montgomery to attend the trial of a friend, he was brutally attacked by police and jailed without cause. Refusing to pay a fine, he was thrown into jail, where he spent several days. Then some anonymous person paid the fine and he was released. This incident created even more sympathy for the black cause.

In September, 1958, as Dr. King sat in a Harlem bookstore autographing *Stride Toward Freedom,* the story of the bus boycott which he had somehow found time to write, a black woman plunged a steel letter-opener into his chest. He was rushed to the Harlem Hospital, where one of the surgeons who removed the weapon remarked that Dr. King had been "within a sneeze" of death. Happily, he recovered completely.

Being pastor of the Montgomery church, added to his

civil-rights activities, proved to be too strenuous, so Dr.
King acceded to his father's wish and became co-pastor
with him of the Atlanta Ebenezer Baptist Church. Living in
Atlanta simplified matters for him, for the main office of the
Southern Christian Leadership Conference, which Dr. King
headed, was located there.

The movement to gain long-denied rights for black
Americans was growing fast. "Freedom riders"—groups of
black and white students mostly from the North—began to
test segregation by riding in southern segregated buses and
staging sit-ins at all-white lunch counters. There were
marches and campaigns to increase the number of black
voters. These activities brought retaliation from whites,
including harassment and even physical violence against
black leaders, which in turn increased the pro-black
demonstrations.

King's effort to desegregate the small city of Albany,
Georgia, was largely unsuccessful; but the opposition
encountered there was nothing compared to that in the larger
city of Birmingham, where police attacked black marchers
with dogs and fire hoses. When Dr. King was jailed
incommunicado, Mrs. King got in touch with the White
House, and President Kennedy himself intervened. Dr.
King was soon allowed to speak with his wife over the
telephone and then released. The tense Birmingham
situation was reported all over America, making newspaper
readers and television viewers increasingly aware of the
social revolution that was going on.

As racial discord grew, so did Dr. King's prestige. To
promote the enactment of a strong civil-rights act, he
organized a March on Washington. At its climax, more than
two thousand blacks and whites, arms linked, marched to
the foot of the Lincoln Memorial. Here, on this day in
August, 1963, Martin Luther King, Jr., spoke of his dream
of a day "when all of God's children—black and white
men, Jews and Gentiles, Protestants and Catholics—will be

able to join hands and sing: 'Free at last! Free at last! Thank God Almighty, we're free at last!' "

Nineteen sixty-four was a memorable year for Martin Luther King, Jr. It started with *Time* magazine's naming him the 1963 Man of the Year, the first black man to be so honored. Calling him "the unchallenged voice of the Negro people," *Time* said he was also "the disquieting conscience of the whites." That spring, civil-rights organizations in Mississippi, Alabama, and Florida, with Dr. King actively involved, carried out a massive drive against segregation. In early June, a Civil Rights Act was passed by Congress and signed into law by President Johnson. In September, Dr. King flew to West Germany at Mayor Willy Brandt's invitation, to speak in West Berlin, then went on to Rome for an audience with Pope Paul. The following month, the news came that he had won the Nobel Peace Prize.

While delighted with the honor, Dr. King insisted it was not intended for him personally, but as "a tribute to the discipline, wise restraint and magnificent courage of the millions of gallant Negroes and white persons of good will who have followed a nonviolent course in seeking to establish a reign of justice and a rule of law across this nation of ours."

On his way to the December 10 ceremonies in Oslo, Dr. King stopped over in London to deliver the evensong sermon at St. Paul's, the first non-Anglican ever to do so. "A spellbinding performance," a newsman called it. In Oslo, Dr. King accepted the award before the Norwegian king and a large and brilliant audience. The next day he spoke in his Nobel address of the not-yet-born peace and brotherhood that were "the essence of the Nobel Prize," and of the need to recognize that "nonviolence is the answer to the crucial political and moral questions of our time—the need for man to overcome oppression and violence without resorting to violence and oppression." And he declared that he had "an abiding faith in America and an audacious faith in the future of mankind."

Back in America, Dr. King continued his nonviolent crusade against "deeply entrenched customs and long-established discriminatory laws." There was fierce opposition from the white population of Selma, Alabama, where he led a campaign to encourage black people to vote. Marchers were turned back by state troopers using tear gas and clubs, and Dr. King was jailed. Released under bond, he continued his drive for Negro registration. Permission was granted for a fifty-mile march from Selma to the state capitol in Montgomery. The thirty thousand marchers, black and white, had the distinction of being led by two Nobel Peace Prize winners—Martin Luther King, Jr., and Ralph Johnson Bunche. It was the most spectacular nonviolent demonstration yet staged of black determination to win racial justice in America.

The two years following the passing of the 1964 Civil Rights Act brought the registration of more black voters, the lifting of many racial restrictions, and a multitude of social changes, both open and subtle. Still, the progress was too slow to suit many young Negroes. They lost patience with Dr. King's policy of moderation and nonviolence and applauded the Black Power movement led by youthful Stokeley Carmichael. There were riots in the Watts district of Los Angeles and in the slum area of Chicago. One commentator declared, "Every major city is sitting on a racial powder keg."

Dr. King, realizing that racism was a northern as well as a southern problem, threw his weight behind Operation Breadbasket in Chicago, a movement intended to emphasize the need for better living conditions and more job opportunities for the black population there. But the level of frustration and despair among the Chicago slum-dwellers was so high that violence broke out, and all efforts to control it were in vain. It was a discouraging experience, although it did succeed in bringing about some improvement in the situation.

The war in Vietnam, Martin Luther King, Jr., believed,

was limiting America's ability to improve conditions for the poor at home, both black and white, and he came out against it. "War is obsolete," he declared as he urged America to exert its moral rather than its military strength. Many of Dr. King's earlier followers criticized him for seeming to engage simultaneously in both the civil-rights and the anti-war movements, and he lost much support. Desperately, he launched a national Operation Breadbasket, but angry young black extremists, much influenced by the Black Power movement, wanted more radical action.

In Memphis, Dr. King led mass meetings and rallies in an effort to win justice for striking garbage workers. To his dismay, for the first time in a march led by him, marchers broke out of line and engaged in acts of violence. Determined to prove the effectiveness of his peaceful methods, he promised to return and lead another march, which he vowed would be nonviolent.

Threats against Dr. King's life had been common for years; he had learned to live with them and not let them interfere with his work. Now these threats increased, but Dr. King's faith held firm. In his final speech, he spoke of having been to the mountaintop and said that even if he did not live to see the promised land, his people would get there.

In Memphis, on April 4, 1968, a sudden shot put an end to the life of Martin Luther King, Jr. Dead at thirty-nine, he had left uncompleted, though on its way to fulfillment, his vision of a peaceful America with justice for all.

1965-1971
14. Good Neighbors All

(United Nations Children's Fund [UNICEF]; Cassin; International Labor Organization [ILO]; Borlaug; Brandt)

The headquarters of the **United Nations Children's Fund** (UNICEF) was in a happy turmoil one October day in 1965. The unexpected news had just arrived that this UN agency had won the "most coveted of all awards," the Nobel Peace Prize. Congratulatory telephone calls and telegrams arrived, and reporters and UN delegates dropped in.

For nearly twenty years, with little fanfare and on a very modest budget, UNICEF had been sending to the needy children of the world food, medicines, and clothing. It had built hospitals and supplied doctors and nurses to staff them. It had sent health experts to help eradicate childhood diseases and instruct in nutrition, sanitation, and healthful living habits. It had provided teachers to tackle the problem of illiteracy. All this had been accomplished by the limited funds contributed by member nations, augmented by Christmas-card sales and nickels and dimes collected by children in their Halloween trick-or-treat forays.

Eleanor Roosevelt had led the way when she created in 1946, the United Nations International Children's Emergency Fund for the relief of the children in war-torn Europe. When, by 1953, the worst of the suffering had been relieved, the UN General Assembly voted to continue the agency for the purpose of "assisting the children of the developing countries who live in the shadow of disease, hunger, ignorance, and poverty." The name was shortened to the United Nations Children's Fund, but the old initials, UNICEF, were retained.

In 1965, when UNICEF received the Nobel Peace Prize, it had nearly two hundred professional field workers, representing seventy-one nations, in thirty-three countries. It had set up more than five hundred projects in over a hundred countries, and had provided services to a billion children. The projects included day centers, health centers, and training schools; and the services included vaccination

against smallpox, medication for malaria and for yaws, treatment for trachoma, and preventive measures against the spread of leprosy. Milk and high-protein foods had been distributed to offset malnutrition, and soaps and disinfectants had been dispensed by the carload to encourage cleanliness. Local governments often cooperated in these projects, and so did local industries and organizations. Sometimes they carried on projects begun by UNICEF, and sometimes, with its help, started their own.

When accepting the Nobel Peace Prize for UNICEF, its director, Henry R. Labousse, said, "The world's future is not just the sum total of its tangibles, but the potential of its children." The award, he added, "acknowledges that the welfare of the children of the world is inseparably linked with the peace of tomorrow's world."

Using the sizable check that accompanied the award, the agency was able to increase the number of day centers, health centers, and training schools, their staffs and equipment. In addition to these ongoing projects, UNICEF has provided help in such disasters as the African drought and the Pakistan floods. Increasing costs have made the financing of this humanitarian work more difficult, but thanks to a dedicated director and devoted staff, and to public support, UNICEF has continued its services "for the love of the children."

In 1966, and again in 1967, the Nobel Peace Prize was not awarded.

The 1968 Nobel Peace Prize went to an eighty-one-year-old French jurist, **René Cassin,** for his lifelong work in promoting human rights. As a young man, Cassin studied law. He fought and was wounded in the First World War, then became a professor of law and a member of the French delegation to the League of Nations. Between the World Wars, he was active in peace efforts and during World War II was associated with Charles de Gaulle's Free French government in England. In 1944, Cassin helped set up the United Nations Educational, Scientific, and Cultural Organization (UNESCO) to promote these objectives on the local level. He was a member of the UN Economic and Social Council's Human Rights Committee, which Eleanor Roosevelt headed, and prepared the preliminary draft of its charter on human rights. After discussion and revision, this charter, called a Universal Declaration of Human Rights, was adopted by the UN General Assembly on December 10, 1948. It marked a turning point in world history, said René Cassin, by providing "an instrument capable of lifting or easing the burden of oppression and injustice in the world." The difficulty, he admitted, was in making use of it, which "involved the responsibility of all of us."

When the Court of Human Rights was established in Strasbourg, France, to hear the appeals of any who believed their human rights were being violated, René Cassin became a member of it and in 1965, its president. He also continued to write and to lecture on human rights.

During his lifetime, Cassin received many honors, including the Grand Cross of the French Legion of Honor, but the honor he treasured most was the Nobel Peace Prize. He had indeed earned it, as the chairman of the Nobel Committee said, by working tirelessly ''for the carrying out of the principles of the Declaration of Human Rights both universally and on the European level.''

The following year, 1969, the Nobel Peace Prize went to the **International Labor Organization,** known as the ILO. Founded under the Versailles Peace Treaty fifty years before, its purpose was to prevent social revolution and

ensure world peace by uniting the workers of the increasingly industrialized world. It aimed to improve labor
conditions, living standards, and labor-management relations. It had a unique tripartite organization, with government, labor, and management each having its own identity
and voting power.

In 1946, backed by more than a hundred member nations,
the ILO transferred its allegiance from the League of
Nations to the United Nations, becoming its first specialized
agency. After staying in the same 1926 headquarters
building in Geneva for nearly fifty years, it moved into a
large, modern building. Its basic principle, however,
remained the same: "Lasting peace can be established only
if it is based on social justice."

With the emergence of the "Third World," the ILO
turned its attention to the increasing problem of worldwide
unemployment. To combat this, it began to give technical
assistance to developing nations, setting up vocational
schools, management-development courses, manpower
planning methods, and social security systems. Through a
staff of two thousand persons, representing a hundred
nationalities, the ILO conducted projects in nearly a
hundred countries.

On December 10, 1969, Mrs. Aase Lionaes, chairman of
the Nobel Committee, when awarding the medal, certificate, and check for around seventy-five thousand to the
ILO, said, "There are few organizations that have
succeeded to the extent that the International Labor
Organization has succeeded in translating into action the
fundamental idea on which it is based." An American
editorial bore out her statement in these words: "A half
century of quiet crusading for social justice underlies the
award. . . . This hardy survivor of agencies for world
cooperation . . . has made its contribution by persistent,
unspectacular dedication to the task of making life more
livable for hundreds of millions of workers and their
families."

The Nobel Peace Prize in 1970 turned the spotlight on agriculture by honoring an American agronomist, **Norman Borlaug.** Raised on an Iowa farm, Borlaug was trained in forestry and plant pathology at the University of Minnesota. In 1944, he went to Mexico as one of a team of four agronomists commissioned by the Rockefeller Institute to try to develop the quality and quantity of Mexican wheat. The aim was to enable Mexico to rely on its own wheat production rather than having to import grain.

Borlaug soon became the director of the wheat-breeding project. In order to test the adaptability of various strains to different climates, he established two experimental areas—one just below the United States border and the other nearly a thousand miles farther south. Through cross pollination, he hoped to develop new strains that would eliminate undesirable qualities and develop desirable ones. After testing many varieties, the team found a disease-resistant Japanese dwarf plant with a broad, stiff stalk, and from this they produced a new strain without the top-heaviness of the old variety. Within ten years' time, it yielded a sufficient quantity of wheat to feed the Mexican people.

Threatened with famine, India and Pakistan became interested in the new dwarf wheat plant. Their governments arranged to experiment with it and found that, with better irrigation and more fertilizer, it thrived in Asia. The wheat harvest was doubled and the threatened famine averted.

Dr. Borlaug was credited with starting a "green revolution." Scientists called his experimenting "an imaginative feat of biological plant engineering." In Mexico, the experimental wheat-breeding was enlarged to apply also to rice and corn. Young men came from many countries to have Dr. Borlaug teach them the secrets of grain cultivation. Occasionally he visited Asia and Africa to check on the various strains of wheat, corn, or rice being developed in the experimental stations he had set up in those countries.

In 1965, Norman Borlaug became director of the International Maize and Wheat Improvement Center,

sponsored by the Rockefeller Foundation, the Ford Foundation, and the Mexican government. A team of scientists from seventeen nations worked in the Mexican experimental fields in an attempt to produce high-yield, high-protein grains to combat hunger and poverty everywhere in the world. Dr. Borlaug called it "a race between food and the exploding population."

Word of the Nobel award came to the agronomist's Mexico City home in October, 1970. Mrs. Borlaug drove forty miles to the experimental field where her husband was working to take the news to him. At first he would not believe it. Then he insisted on finishing his day's work before going home to meet the reporters waiting to interview him. After admitting he was greatly pleased with the honor, he said he would not stop long to bask in it, for while the green revolution might temporarily stave off mass starvation, there was much to be done in many countries.

In presenting the award, the Committee chairman credited Dr. Borlaug with creating "a technological breakthrough which makes it possible to abolish hunger in the developing countries in the course of a few years." But Dr. Borlaug said that only population control could win the battle of hunger in the world. We must, he said, "strike a proper balance between population and food resources."

Scientists were especially pleased with the favorable recognition the award brought to the green revolution. It showed, they said, "the extent to which scientific effort can constructively influence human conditions and prospects for peace and security."

To understand the awarding of the 1971 Nobel Peace Prize to **Willy Brandt,** one must be familiar with the widespread political unrest and tensions existing in Europe in the 1960s. The two-way division of Germany and the Soviet domination over the eastern European nations affected hundreds of thousands. Berlin, Germany's largest city, located in the eastern, Russian-controlled part of the country, was divided politically. Its western section, West Berlin, was controlled by World War II Allies Britain, France, and the United States; and the eastern section, East Berlin, by the Russians.

Willy Brandt had fled Germany in the first year of the Hitler rule because of his Social Democratic Party allegiance. He spent the war years in exile in Scandinavia. There he worked with the Norwegians in resisting the Nazi invaders of their land and with the resistance fighters in Germany. Brandt became well acquainted with danger, imprisonment, and narrow escapes.

After the Second World War, he returned to his

homeland, determined to dedicate his life to "the reconstruction of a new Germany" and "the rehabilitation of
European and German democracy." He earned a meager
living as a journalist in West Berlin while struggling to
revive the old Social Democratic Party. Soon he was editing
the party paper. With his Norwegian wife, he suffered
through the 1948–49 Soviet blockade of West Berlin. He
called the city's rescue through the Allied airlift "a miracle
of technique, organization, and machines."

Willy Brandt's natural ability, integrity, energy, and
determination gradually made him an important political
figure in West Berlin. He tried to establish by peaceful
means "a regulated side-by-side existence" between
politically separated East and West Berlin. When West
Germany became the Federal Republic of Germany, with its
capital at Bonn, Brandt was elected one of eight representatives from West Berlin to the government's first
Parliament. Because of West Berlin's location in the eastern
(Russian) part of Germany, it became a sort of isolated
city-state. Brandt tried to strengthen the ties between the
city and the West German national government. At the same
time, as a member of the West Berlin House of
Representatives, and after a time its president, he worked
with the city's mayor, Ernest Reuter, to improve employ-
ment and living standards in West Berlin.

Conditions in Russian-controlled East Berlin were far
worse than in West Berlin. In 1953, East Berlin workers
staged an uprising that was brutally put down by Russian
tanks and troops. The East Berliners "did not only rebel
against insufficient wages," said Willy Brandt, "they
wanted freedom." But he insisted that the German problem
must be solved peacefully.

Three years later, when freedom fighters in Hungary
rebelled against Russia, Brandt did more than speak out. A
crowd of indignant West Berliners, demonstrating to show
their sympathy with the rebelling Hungarians, started to
march toward East Berlin. Brandt realized they might

provoke Soviet troops stationed there and that this could result in war. Using all his powers of persuasion, he induced the mob to change the direction of its march and to continue its demonstration at a West Berlin memorial to the victims of Stalinism. There, with some of their energy dissipated, he led the demonstrators in patriotic songs and then reasoned with them. Learning that another mob was actually marching toward East Berlin, he and his wife left the first gathering and rushed to where the second set of marchers was. Again he was able to control the protesters, getting them ''to sing defiantly the German national anthem" and then to listen to reason. By his intelligent and daring action, Brandt prevented a clash that might well have meant the end of West Berlin.

Ernest Reuter, the mayor of West Berlin, died suddenly and soon so also did the elderly official who succeeded him. By an overwhelming vote, the West Berlin House of Representatives elected Willy Brandt to be city mayor. Brandt governed West Berlin ably and energetically. He worked for better relations between East and West Berlin and also for a closer relationship between the city and the West German government, the Federal Republic of Germany. "The fate of West Berlin," he insisted, "cannot be separated from the fate of all other Germans."

Increasingly Brandt craved the larger responsibilities and opportunities of a closer connection with the West German government. The country's policies, he felt, were too conservative and its officials too content with things as they were and too hostile toward their Communist neighbor states. After serving for almost ten years, from 1957 to 1966, as mayor of West Berlin, Brandt won the post of vice chancellor and foreign minister in the Federal Republic. He spoke strongly on behalf of the nuclear non-proliferation treaty. He proposed a four-power conference "not to end Germany's division, but to make the *status quo* more bearable." He recommended a program of reconciliation between West Germany and the Communist nations to the east and, to his satisfaction, actually established diplomatic relations with several of them.

Brandt's efforts toward better relations between East and West Germany, however, met with little success. Walter Ulbricht, president of the German Democratic Republic (East Germany), insisted on full recognition of his country. He rejected all offers of "qualified recognition," such as Brandt's "small steps" suggestions of exchanging newspapers and granting more border passes.

In 1969, Willy Brandt achieved his ambition to become Chancellor of the Federal Republic of Germany. Turning his attention from East Germany to its Russian sponsor, he succeeded in arranging a nonaggression treaty with the Soviet Union and also with Poland. The western world called the signing of these treaties "a formidable contribution to East-West reconciliation," and "the beginning of a new era."

When Chancellor Brandt was told that he was a leading candidate for the 1971 Nobel Peace Prize, he demurred, saying that his peace-making policies were still incomplete. But the Nobel Peace Prize Committee selected Willy Brandt unanimously. On a day in October, 1971, the president of the West German *Bundstag* (Parliament) "clanged his handbell," bringing the House to sudden silence. As he announced the honor that had come to Willy Brandt, there was deafening applause. Amid the noisy acclaim, Chancellor Brandt declared himself deeply moved, and promised to try to make himself worthy of the honor.

Chancellor Brandt was the first head of a government to receive the Nobel Peace Prize since Woodrow Wilson in 1915; he was also the first German to win the award since Carl von Ossietzky in 1935. Norway had not forgotten that it had been Willy Brandt's home during the Hitler regime in Germany. Now his many Norwegian friends, hailing him as "our own Willy," welcomed him back to receive the high award at the December 10 ceremonies in Oslo.

The Committee cited Chancellor Brandt for contributing to the relaxation of tension between East and West by "stretching out his hand in reconciliation toward former enemy countries." Specifically mentioned were his signing the treaty to prevent the spread of nuclear weapons, the nonaggression treaties with Poland and the Soviet Union, his efforts to extend the membership of the Common Market and, as mayor of West Berlin, his attempt to obtain for his people "the fundamental human rights of personal security and full freedom of movement."

In his Nobel address, which he delivered in flawless Norwegian, Willy Brandt took his stand firmly with all those who, "regardless of their positions, are striving with all their might to liberate the world from wars and to organize a Europe of peace." He was proud, he said, that in the difficult search for a lasting peace, the Federal Republic of Germany "had not been a sleeping partner but a driving force," and he pledged his word that "this will remain."

Journalists, while agreeing that the award was an impressive tribute to Brandt, insisted that it was still too soon to assess the "Peace Chancellor's" policy of seeking reconciliation with the Communist nations of eastern Europe. That verdict, they said, would have to be judged by the yardstick of history.

This yardstick was not altogether kind to Willy Brandt. For a time, his policy of reconciliation was warmly praised. In 1973, Soviet Party Chief Breshnev made an unprecedented visit to Bonn, where he stated that a bond had been forged between the Soviet Union and the Federated Republic of Germany "for building a stable edifice of good neighborly relations." But early in 1974, Brandt was beset by political troubles—a series of strikes, the splitting of his Social Democratic Party, and widespread criticism that he had given the Russians too much in exchange for too little.

A few months later, the disclosure that a close personal aide to Willy Brandt was in reality an East German spy caused Chancellor Brandt to resign. Some regarded this act of resignation as "an example of integrity"; others saw it as an acknowledgement of political negligence. The ex-Chancellor wrote his version of the government scandal in a book whose English title is *Beyond This Day*. He continued to serve as head of the Social Democratic Party and to play an important, though unofficial, role in the domestic and foreign affairs of West Germany.

Whatever Willy Brandt's future, his accomplishments as mayor of West Berlin and as Chancellor of the Federated Republic of Germany will not be forgotten, nor will his courageous "step by step" and "good neighbor" attempts to gain a more secure peace in Europe and in the world.

1972-1975
15. "No Moratorium in the Quest for a Peaceful World"

(Kissinger and Tho; MacBride and Sato; Sakharov)

The Nobel Peace Prize was not awarded in 1972.

In 1973, **Henry Kissinger,** United States Secretary of State, and **Le Duc Tho** of the North Vietnam government, won the Nobel Peace Prize. The joint award, which recognized the negotiations to bring about a cease-fire in Vietnam, was much criticized. It was said that the agreement made by the negotiators had never been fully implemented and that fighting in Vietnam continued. Tho, the Paris paper *Le Monde* pointed out, had always been committed to revolution, and Kissinger had supported the Vietnam war, including the bombing of Hanoi. "Hawks who blamed North Vietnam for the hostilities were outraged at the choice of Tho; doves who thought the war could have been ended much sooner were angry at the choice of Kissinger."

The Nobel Peace Prize Committee's five members had also disagreed. The threat of two of them to resign from the Committee created something of a political crisis in the Norwegian Parliament, but the decision of the majority of three stood firm.

When notified, Kissinger declared himself much moved by the award; Tho, after a "stony silence," refused it, stating as his reason the violation of the cease-fire by South Vietnam and the United States. He would consider

189

accepting the award, he said, "when the Paris agreement on Vietnam is respected, guns are silenced, and peace is really restored in Vietnam." (A year later, in November, 1974, the director of the Nobel Institute announced that Le Duc Tho, by failing to meet the deadline for formally accepting the award, had forfeited his share of the prize money.)

Defenders of the award said that, more than the men involved, the award recognized the "art of negotiation itself: the process of ending a war and laying the groundwork for peace." Certainly the negotiations between Le Duc Tho and Henry Kissinger had been long and difficult.

The two men met first in Paris in August, 1969, when they were commissioned by their governments, North Vietnam and the United States, to work out secretly an acceptable plan to end the war between North and South Vietnam. Over a period of three years, while the fighting in South Vietnam continued, Kissinger and Tho met many times in an effort to find a way through the complex situation. Though outwardly polite and always parting with smiles, the two had little confidence in each other. Persistence and skillful diplomacy finally resulted in a much-revised agreement, signed in January, 1973. It provided for taking American troops out of the conflict, returning American prisoners of war, and making the first steps toward a final peace.

Newsmen found it difficult to learn much about Le Duc Tho. He had been an active revolutionary since 1928, had organized guerrilla movements against the French, whose colony North Vietnam then was, and as a result had spent seven years in prison. Later he joined the Indo-Chinese Communist Party, was elected to its central committee, and achieved a top-ranking post in the North Vietnamese government. It was said that never in his entire life had he known tranquility.

In contrast to the meager information on Le Duc Tho, that on Henry Kissinger was voluminous. At fifteen, he left

Germany with his family to escape the growing anti-Semitism of the Hitler regime. In New York, Henry soon became a straight-A high school student, despite his foreign-language handicap. He worked as a delivery boy and was studying to become an accountant when, at nineteen, he was drafted into the United States Army. In the closing months of World War II, after becoming a naturalized U.S. citizen, he was sent to Germany. There, because of his intelligence and his fluency in German, he was assigned to administer one of the captured German cities. Young Kissinger performed the job well, being both firm and sympathetic. "We have not come here for revenge," he told the German people. Before he ended his army career, Kissinger was a captain and had been offered an instructorship in the command school.

Instead, Henry Kissinger went to college. Granted a scholarship, he earned his B.A. degree from Harvard in three years, then won his M.A., and finally his Ph.D. He had, one of his professors said, "an unusual and original mind . . . with a feeling for political philosophy." His special interest was nineteenth-century European history. During the summers, he directed the Harvard International Seminar, a program in which outstanding foreign students came to Cambridge to discuss politics, philosophy, and history. The Army Operations Research Office made Kissinger a consultant and sent him to Korea to observe the effects of the military occupation.

Young Dr. Kissinger accepted a position with the Council on Foreign Relations, which took him to New York. There he made the acquaintance of important persons in the fields of government, diplomacy, industry, and journalism. Being methodical and industrious, Kissinger found time to write a book entitled *Nuclear Weapons and Foreign Policy;* it attracted the attention of both scholars and general readers.

Beginning as lecturer in Harvard's department of government, by 1962, Kissinger was a full professor with tenure. He had remained with the Council of Foreign Relations and, in addition, directed a special studies project set up by Nelson Rockefeller. This further enlarged his circle of intellectual acquaintances. In the early sixties, Kissinger wrote many articles for scholarly periodicals and two more books on American foreign policy. In them he expressed the opinion that the national defense policy was outmoded.

In 1965, Henry Cabot Lodge, then ambassador to South Vietnam, requested that Henry Kissinger be appointed as consultant to the Department of State and be sent to South Vietnam to report on the military and political situation there. His "brilliant analysis" triggered a second visit which confirmed his earlier opinion that the primary issues in the Vietnam war were "not military but political and psychological."

During the last year of the Johnson administration, Dr. Kissinger made his first acquaintance with secret diplomacy. While in Paris as a State Department consultant, he became a go-between in a semiofficial approach to North Vietnam's Premier Ho Chi Minh. Though nothing came of this, it was a valuable experience for Kissinger.

The following year, the newly elected President Nixon appointed Kissinger to his National Security Council and charged him with making it a "centralized, calibrated, policy-making" organization. This Henry Kissinger did, choosing his staff on the basis of ability rather than politics, and inaugurating a policy of global strategy based on "linkage" between distant events and on anticipating crises instead of meeting them unprepared.

Ending the Vietnam war honorably, Dr. Kissinger declared, was "essential for the peace of the world." There was no purely military solution, he said; peace must come largely through negotiation. And so, in 1969, he began the secret Paris meetings with North Vietnam's Le Duc Tho. The talks brought many disappointments and frequent miscalculations, it seemed, by each side, though Kissinger said that at times he could "almost taste peace."

Other problems also demanded Dr. Kissinger's attention. Among them were events in the Far and Middle East, the Nixon journey to China, and the Moscow summit meeting. Yet he did not neglect the Tho negotiations, and eventually the time came when he announced elatedly, "We've got a deal!" This day, however, was followed by bad moments and weeks of delay caused by ambiguities in the agreement, South Vietnamese objections, changes in White House directives, and Tho's sudden hostility. Even in the spring and summer of 1973, after the agreement had been signed, cease-fire violations persisted, as Tho noted.

Dr. Kissinger became the U.S. Secretary of State in September, 1973, a month before he learned he had won the Nobel Peace Prize. That fall the Arab-Israeli war occurred, and Kissinger flew to the Middle East. He also paid his second visit to China. On December 10, as Secretary of State, he had to be in Brussels to attend a NATO Council meeting and so could not go to Oslo to receive the award in person. In his acceptance speech, read by the United States ambassador to Norway, Dr. Kissinger said he believed the award honored a purpose more than a person, and symbolized the quest of peace rather than its achievement. "Peace," he declared, "cannot be achieved by one man or one nation. . . . If lasting peace is to come, it will be the accomplishment of all mankind."

Dr. Kissinger's share of the prize money amounted to $63,000; he used it to establish a scholarship fund for children of American servicemen killed or missing in action in Vietnam. (A year later, the *New York Times* stated that from eight to ten scholarships would be awarded the following spring.)

Continuing as Secretary of State under President Ford, Dr. Kissinger pursued his program of almost constant worldwide travel in an effort to promote more peaceful conditions in the fast changing world. As "principal architect of American foreign policy," he has been both highly praised and severely criticized. It has been noted, however, that always his words and his actions have seemed consistent with his "strong sense of public duty, his attachment to power, and perhaps most of all, his determination to do whatever he can to preserve the laboriously constructed underpinning of his 'structure of peace.'" For, as he has stated: "There can be no moratorium in the quest for a peaceful world."

Many believed the Nobel Peace Prize would not be given in 1974 because of the widespread criticism of the award to Henry Kissinger and Le Duc Tho. But in October, the Committee announced the joint winners of the 1974 award—the Irish Sean MacBride, United Nations Commissioner of South-West Africa (Namibia), and Eisaku Sato, former Premier of Japan.

Sean MacBride had been a founder and the chairman of Amnesty International, an organization created to work for the release of political prisoners. He had headed the Permanent International Peace Bureau in Geneva, the world's oldest peace organization and the recipient of the 1910 Nobel Peace Prize, and had worked for many years to build human rights safeguards into various international agreements.

When MacBride was a boy, his Irish father had been executed by the British for his part in the 1916 Irish Easter Rising, and his mother had been imprisoned in London. As soon as Sean was out of the Paris and Dublin schools in which he was educated, he joined the Irish Republican Army, where he soon became an officer and later chief of staff.

With maturity, Sean MacBride saw the futility of war as a method of solving the world's problems. He became a lawyer, entered the Irish Parliament, and exerted his influence to promote peaceful relations with other countries. As Minister for External Affairs, he took part in international conferences; he also became active in many international organizations.

Because of his industriousness, his talent, and his legal background, the United Nations chose Sean MacBride to be its commissioner for South-West Africa. Before the Second World War, this country had been a German colony; following the war, it was administered by the Union of South Africa under a mandate from the United Nations. After many years, the UN ordered South Africa to end its mandate and grant South-West Africa its independence. South Africa did not wish to do this, partly because of Namibia's potentially valuable mineral resources. Mac-Bride, having been born in Africa, had a rather personal interest in the problem and took very seriously the responsibility given him by the UN. He saw as his main objective the education of blacks in Namibia's white-dominated population and their training in administrative skills in preparation for self-government.

At the December 10, 1974, ceremonies, the chairman of the Nobel Peace Prize Committee said that both recipients of the year's award had contributed "each in his own way to securing peace. Their efforts have come to areas that in our time are central to the work of peace."

Eisaku Sato was honored for his contribution to the political stability of the Pacific area. Never before had a Japanese won the Nobel Peace Prize, and most of the Japanese people were elated at the honor. A few, however, pointed out that when Mr. Sato was Premier of Japan—from 1964 to 1972—he had at first criticized the non-nuclear power treaty and that, after it was signed, he made no effort to have it ratified by the Japanese Diet (Parliament).

An unhappy note was the admission of the wealthy chairman of a Japanese construction company that he had waged a year-long campaign to influence the Nobel Peace Prize Committee to select Mr. Sato. To accomplish this, he had arranged for Mr. Sato's speeches to be published under the title *In Quest of Peace and Freedom,* and he had also written numerous important persons urging them to support Sato's candidacy. In defense, he said, "I thought it was just about time to get the prize for a Japanese, whose country has pursued peace under the no-war constitution, rejecting nuclear arms." The Nobel Committee, as usual, paid no attention to this flurry.

Eisaku Sato was known as a cautious and conservative politician whose career had been one of ups and downs. Once, indicted for bribe-taking, he had dropped out of sight for almost a decade, then was reinstated in his Liberal Democratic Party and made its head. After being elected Premier of Japan, Mr. Sato was responsible for arranging the return to Japan of the American-held island of Okinawa. He also established a policy of reconciliation with countries of Asia, setting up diplomatic relations with South Korea and making economic pacts with several Asian countries. In

addition to leading his country into an active Asian role, Sato signed the nonproliferation treaty prohibiting the spread of nuclear weapons and pledging Japan to abstain from their use.

When Sato's political fortunes again seemed to take a downward turn, he resigned the premiership; it was as a private citizen that he received the Nobel Peace Prize.

The 1975 Nobel Peace Prize went to **Andrei Sakharov,** Soviet scientist turned humanitarian. He was the first Russian to win the Nobel Peace Prize, but the honor was not appreciated by the Soviet Union. Though at one time the Russian government had favored Sakharov, he was now considered its enemy.

During the late forties and early fifties, Dr. Sakharov played an important part in the Soviet Union's development of nuclear weapons, a part so important that he was often called "the father of the hydrogen bomb." But as Dr.

Sakharov began to realize the threat of nuclear war posed by the bomb, his conscience troubled him. He wrote about war and peace, technological advances, dictatorship and freedom in a book he called *Progress, Coexistence, and Intellectual Freedom.* He also became active in promoting human-rights causes, in working to end religious persecution and censorship, and in securing amnesty for political prisoners.

Dr. Sakharov's criticism of his country's policies displeased the Soviet government. Although he was not brought to trial, he was barred from his laboratory and from other means of doing scientific research. He was also ostracized by most of his associates and slandered by the Soviet press. In spite of this, Andrei Sakharov courageously continued to battle against what he considered wrong in the Soviet political and social system and to argue for a reduction of armaments and for peaceful coexistence with other countries.

The announcement that the 1975 Nobel Peace Prize was to go to Andrei Sakharov brought bitter attacks from Soviet newspapers. They called the decision a "political ploy contrary to the interests of peace and East-West detente" and denounced Dr. Sakharov as an "antipatriot" who had "taken a stand against his own country." A third of Dr. Sakharov's colleagues in the renowned Soviet Academy of Sciences, to which he still belonged, signed a statement calling the award a "blasphemy against the noble ideals cherished by all of us of humanism, peace, justice, and friendship between peoples of all countries." Dr. Sakharov's activities, they declared, were "aimed to undermine peace, peaceful and equal relations between states, and inspire distrust between peoples."

Disregarding this blast, Dr. Sakharov expressed his hope that the award would "support the battle for human rights" in the Soviet Union, and he renewed his plea for an amnesty for political prisoners.

After some weeks of silence, the Soviet authorities

refused to grant Dr. Sakharov permission to go to Oslo to accept the award, stating that he might give away secret information concerning the hydrogen bomb. It happened that Dr. Sakharov's wife was in Italy for eye surgery and treatment; she flew to Oslo to stand in for her husband at the December 10 ceremony. It was attended by King Olaf V and his cabinet ministers, members of the Parliament, diplomats and important persons from many countries—but none from the Soviet Union or from any Soviet-controlled countries.

Mrs. Aase Lionaes, chairman of the Nobel Peace Prize Committee, said she "deeply deplored that Andrei Sakharov has been prevented from being present here

today.'' She emphasized the entire independence of the
Nobel Committee and said its work ''was not influenced in
any way by fear or dictated by convenience or oppor-
tunism.'' Calling Dr. Sakharov ''one of the great champions of human rights in our age,'' she read the more than
usually detailed citation, which began: ''Uncompromisingly
and forcefully, Dr. Sakharov has fought not only against the
abuse of power and violation of human dignity in all its
forms, but he has with equal vigor fought for the ideal of a
state founded on the principle of justice for all.''

Mrs. Sakharov, after accepting for her husband the
medal, certificate, and check for $143,000, read his
statement, which was then translated from the Russian into
Norwegian. Under the circumstances, he wrote, he considered it ''an act of intellectual courage and great equity to
grant the award to a man whose ideas do not coincide with
official concepts of the leadership of a big and powerful
state.''

Outside the hall where Dr. Sakharov's words were being
read, young people were marching in a torchlight procession to show their support of Andrei Sakharov and his fight
for individual freedom. This tenth of December was a very
special day—the seventy-fifth anniversary of the first
awarding of the Swedish inventor's great legacy to the
world, his extraordinary plan for the annual recognition of
''those who have conferred the most benefit on mankind.''

16. After Seventy-five Years

"I have a desire to create a spiritual family which, down through the ages, shall be enabled to give their best services to humanity through the agency of my money." This is what Alfred Nobel told a Swedish engineer friend who was witnessing his will in the Swedish Club in Paris in November, 1895.

How well, one wonders, has Alfred Nobel's purpose been accomplished by his remarkable will in the first seventy-five years it has been in effect? And how content would its maker be with the history of the Nobel Peace Prize over its first three quarters of a century?

The skill with which the Nobel Foundation was set up, and the faithfulness of its officials in carrying out his instructions, would surely impress Alfred Nobel. And the five members of the Nobel Peace Prize Committee, appointed by the Norwegian Parliament as Nobel directed, have from the beginning worked intelligently and conscientiously in making their selection from the candidates proposed. When, as has happened nineteen times, none of the candidates seemed to the Committee to merit the award, it has been withheld.

The fact that, of all the prizes he specified, the one for peace has been the most highly regarded would, one believes, be especially pleasing to Alfred Nobel. He would be happy to hear it called "the world's highest humanitarian award," and "the greatest honor a man can receive in this world."

As a good businessman, Alfred Nobel would no doubt be interested to learn that, thanks to the Swedish Nobel Fund's astute investments, in seventy-five years the money value of each prize increased by 200 percent. He might, however, be a little disturbed that the press and public sometimes seemed to place more emphasis on the financial reward than on the recipient's service to humanity.

In view of his desire "to encourage great minds to continued activity in the service of humanity," Nobel might question the frequency with which the Nobel Peace Prize has been awarded to persons almost at the end of their working days. But he could take some comfort from these statements of younger recipients: "This great reward binds me fast to the work I have begun" (Fridtjof Nansen). "[The award puts on me] a high and binding obligation" (Willy Brandt). "I cannot forget that the Nobel Prize for Peace was also a commission—a commission to work harder than I had ever worked before for 'the brotherhood of man'" (Martin Luther King, Jr.).

Alfred Nobel would certainly marvel at the variety represented in his "spiritual family." There are professional promoters of peace, lawyers and jurists, diplomats, statesmen, labor leaders, social workers, editors, doctors, professors, scientists, men of the cloth, and even a soldier. His instruction that "no consideration whatever shall be given to the nationality of the candidate, so that the most worthy shall receive the prize," has been carefully followed. Nobel Peace Prize winners have come from twenty different countries—Switzerland, France, Great Britain, Sweden, Norway, Denmark, Germany, Austria, Italy, Belgium, the Netherlands, the United States (the most numerous), Canada, Argentina, French Equatorial Africa, the Union of South Africa, North Vietnam, Japan, Ireland, and the Soviet Union.

The Nobel Peace Prize winners' methods of trying to achieve a peaceful world have been as varied as their backgrounds. Some have favored the paths of diplomacy, mediation, and arbitration; others have insisted that peace will come only through disarmament. Humanitarians have worked for a peaceful world through efforts to wipe out world hunger, create jobs, improve housing conditions, educate children.

It may need a longer yardstick of history than seventy-five years to determine the real significance of Albert

Nobel's plan of annually conferring honor and substantial financial reward on champions of peace. No one can estimate the number of persons who may be influenced each year by this award to put their weight behind the ongoing struggle to achieve a world of peace and security. Impressive as the first seventy-five years of the Nobel Peace Prize have been, it may be that in the next three quarters of a century, this award will play an even greater part in convincing the inhabitants of this nuclear-age world that, as another scientist, Albert Einstein, said, "Peace is the greatest of all causes."

Winners of the Nobel Peace Prize, 1901-1975

1901   Jean Henri Dunant (1828–1910) (Swiss)
      and Frédéric Passy (1822–1912) (French)
1902   Élie Ducommun (1833–1906) (Swiss)
      and Albert Gobat (1843–1914) (Swiss)
1903   William Randal Cremer (1838–1908) (British)
1904   Institute of International Law (est. 1873)
1905   Bertha Kinsky von Suttner (1843–1914) (Austrian)
1906   Theodore Roosevelt (1858–1919) (American)
1907   Ernesto Teodoro Moneta (1833–1918) (Italian)
      and Louis Renault (1843–1918) (French)
1908   Klas Pontus Arnoldson (1844–1916) (Swedish)
      and Fredrik Bajer (1837–1922) (Danish)
1909   Auguste Beernaert (1829–1912) (Belgian)
      and Paul d'Estournelles de Constant
      (1852–1924) (French)
1910   Permanent International Bureau of Peace (est. 1891)
1911   Tobias Asser (1838–1913) (Dutch)
      and Alfred Fried (1864–1921) (Austrian)
1912   Elihu Root (1845–1937) (American)
1913   Henri Lafontaine (1854–1943) (Belgian)
1914   No Award
1915   No Award
1916   No Award
1917   International Committee of the Red Cross (est. 1863)
1918   No Award
1919   Woodrow Wilson (1856–1924) (American)
1920   Léon Bourgeois (1851–1925) (French)
1921   Hjalmar Branting (1860–1925) (Swedish)
      and Christian Lange (1869–1938) (Norwegian)
1922   Fridtjof Nansen (1861–1930) (Norwegian)
1923   No Award

1924   No Award
1925   Charles Dawes (1865–1951) (American) and
      Sir Austen Chamberlain (1863–1937) (British)
1926   Aristide Briand (1862–1932) (French)
      and Gustav Stresemann (1878–1929) (German)
1927   Ferdinand Buisson (1841–1932) (French)
      and Ludwig Quidde (1858–1941) (German)
1928   No Award
1929   Frank Billings Kellogg (1856–1937) (American)
1930   Nathan Söderblom (1866–1931) (Swedish)
1931   Nicholas Murray Butler (1862–1947)
      (American) and Jane Addams
      (1860–1935) (American)
1932   No Award
1933   Sir Norman Angell (1874–1967) (British)
1934   Arthur Henderson (1863–1935) (British)
1935   Carl von Ossietzky (1889–1938) (German)
1936   Carlos Saavedra Lamas (1880–1959) (Argentinean)
1937   Lord Robert Cecil (1864–1958) (British)
1938   Nansen International Office for Refugees (est. 1930)
1939   No Award
1940   No Award
1941   No Award
1942   No Award
1943   No Award
1944   International Committee of the Red Cross (est. 1863)
1945   Cordell Hull (1871–1955) (American)
1946   Emily Greene Balch (1867–1961) (American)
      and John Raleigh Mott (1865–1955) (American)
1947   The British Friends Service Council (est. 1850)
      and The American Friends Service
      Committee (est. 1917)
1948   No Award
1949   Lord John Boyd Orr (1880–1971) (British)
1950   Ralph Johnson Bunche (1903–1971) (American)
1951   Léon Jouhaux (1879–1954) (French)
1952   Albert Schweitzer (1875–1965) (Alsatian)

1953   George Catlett Marshall (1880–1959) (American)
1954   Office of the United Nations High Commissioner
          for Refugees (est. 1951)
1955   No Award
1956   No Award
1957   Lester Bowles Pearson (1897–1972) (Canadian)
1958   Dominique Georges Henri Pire (1910–   ) (Belgian)
1959   Philip John Noel-Baker (1889–   ) (British)
1960   Albert John Luthuli (1898–1967) (South African)
1961   Dag Hammarskjöld (1905–1961) (Swedish)
1962   Linus Carl Pauling (1901–   ) (American)
1963   International Committee of the Red Cross (est. 1863)
          and The League of Red Cross Societies
          (est. 1919)
1964   Martin Luther King, Jr. (1929–1968) (American)
1965   United Nations Children's Fund (UNICEF) (est. 1946)
1966   No Award
1967   No Award
1968   René Cassin (1887–1976) (French)
1969   International Labor Organization (ILO) (est. 1919)
1970   Norman Borlaug (1914–   ) (American)
1971   Willy Brandt (1914–   ) (German)
1972   No Award
1973   Henry Kissinger (1924–   ) (American)
          and Le Duc Tho (1912–   ) (Vietnamese)
1974   Sean MacBride (1904–   ) (Irish) and
          Eisaku Sato (1901–   ) (Japanese)
1975   Andrei Sakharov (1921–   ) (Russian)

Index

Addams, Jane, 91, 94-99
African National Congress, 151, 152
American Friends Service Committee, 115-17
American Red Cross, 111
Angell, Sir Norman, 99-101
Arbitration, 18, 29, 38, 40, 46, 48, 51-52, 62
Arnoldson, Klas, 57
Asser, Tobias, 60

Bajer, Fredrik, 57-58
Balch, Emily, 113-14
Beernaert, Auguste, 58-59
Bernadotte, Count Folke, 120, 122-23, 126
Borlaug, Norman, 181-83
Bourgeois, Léon, 74-75
Brandt, Willy, 183-88, 202
Branting, Hjalmar, 75-76
Briand, Aristide, 85-86
British Friends Service Council, 115
Buisson, Ferdinand, 87
Bunche, Ralph Johnson, 120-26
Butler, Nicholas Murray, 88-89, 91-93

Carnegie Endowment for International Peace, 48-49, 63, 91-92

Cassin, René, 178-79
Cecil, Lord Robert, 107-9
Chamberlain, Sir Austen, 85
Civil rights. See Human rights

Cremer, William Randal, 28, 38-40, 52

Dawes, Charles, 83-85
Dawes Plan, 84, 85
Disarmament, 44, 77, 102, 165
Ducommun, Élie, 36-37, 59
Dunant, Jean Henri, 27, 29-36, 46, 111

Einstein, Albert, 163, 203
Estournelles, Paul d', 59
Explosives, 12-14, 15, 17, 163-64

Ford, Henry, 97
Fried, Alfred, 49, 61
Friends, 115-17

Geneva Convention, 33, 56
Gobat, Albert, 37, 60

Hague Conference (1899), 41, 45-46; (1907), 48, 53-54
Hague Tribunal, 51-52, 54
Hammarskjöld, Dag, 155-61
Henderson, Arthur, 102-3
Hull, Cordell, 111-12
Hull House, 94-95, 98, 99
Human rights, 151, 154, 170-72, 174, 178, 187, 198, 200

Institute of International Law, 40-41
International Bureau of Peace, 64
International Committee of the Red Cross, 65-66, 109-11, 166
Internationalism, 64, 76, 77, 85, 91, 92
International Labor Organization, 179-80
International Red Cross, 29, 33, 35-36
Interparliamentary Union, 40, 77

Jouhaux, Léon, 127-28

Kellogg-Briand Pact, 88-89, 92
Kellogg, Frank Billings, 88-89, 92
King, Martin Luther, Jr., 167-75, 202
Kinsky, Bertha, 16. See also Suttner, Bertha Kinsky von
Kissinger, Henry, 189-94

Lafontaine, Henry, 63-64
Lamas. See Saavedra Lamas
Lange, Christian, 65, 76-77, 142
League of Nations, 70-73, 74-75, 79-80, 81, 109
League of Red Cross Societies, 166
Lilljequist, Rudolf, 21, 23
Locarno Pact, 85
Luthuli, Albert John, 148-54

MacBride, Sean, 194, 195-96
Marshall, George Catlett, 139-40
Moneta, Ernesto Teodoro, 55-56
Mott, John Raleigh, 114

Nansen, Fridtjof, 77-82, 202
Nansen International Office for Refugees, 109, 141

Nobel, Alfred, 11-21; and Bertha Kinsky von Suttner, 16, 17, 18, 42, 44-45; and explosives, 12-17, 19, 20; and peace, 18-19; and prizes, 18-19, 20, 21-26; will, 19, 20, 21-26, 45, 201-3
Nobel, Emanuel, 21, 22-23, 24-25, 47
Nobel, Emil, 12, 13
Nobel Foundation, 25, 26, 201
Nobel, Hjalmar, 19, 21, 22, 23, 24, 25
Nobel, Immanuel, 11, 12, 13, 14
Nobel Institute, 65, 76
Nobel, Ludwig, 11, 12, 16, 20
Nobel Peace Prize Committee, 26, 47, 55, 65, 104, 189, 201
Nobel Peace Prize winners, 202
Nobel, Robert, 11, 12, 16, 20
Noel-Baker, Philip John, 147-48
North Atlantic Treaty Organization, 142
Norwegian Parliament, 22, 23-24, 25, 26
Nuclear arms, 163-64, 165
Nutrition, 118-19, 181-83

Orr, Lord John Boyd, 118-19
Ossietzky, Carl von, 103-6

Palestine, partition of, 122-24
Paris Peace Conference, 70-71, 98
Passy, Frédéric, 27-29, 39, 46
Pauling, Linus, 161-65
Peace, 18-19, 22, 44, 45, 47, 125-26, 128, 137, 145, 180, 194, 203
Pearson, Lester Bowles, 141-45
Permanent International Bureau of Peace, 29, 36, 37, 59
Pire, Dominique Goerges Henri, 145-47

Quidde, Ludwig, 87-88

Red Cross, 29, 33, 35-36, 56, 65-66, 109-11, 166
Refugees, 80, 81, 109, 140-41

Renault, Louis, 56
Roosevelt, Theodore, 47, 51-55
Root, Elihu, 62-63, 91-92
Russo-Japanese War mediation, 52-53

Saavedra Lamas, Carlos, 106-7
Sakharov, Andrei, 197-200
Sato, Eisaku, 194, 196-97
Schweitzer, Albert, 129-38
Söderblom, Nathan, 21, 89-90, 133-34
Sohlman, Ragnar, 19, 21, 23-25
Solferino, battle of, 30-32
Stresemann, Gustav, 85, 86
Suttner, Bertha Kinsky von, 17, 18-19, 42-49, 61. *See also* Kinsky, Bertha

Tho, Le Duc, 189-90

United Nations, 120-22, 124, 126, 156-61
United Nations Children's Fund, 176-78
United Nations High Commissioner for Refugees, Office of the, 140-41
United Nations Peace Supervisory Force, 144, 158
United Nations Relief and Rehabilitation Administration, 109

Versailles Peace Treaty, 61, 70-72, 82, 85, 105
Vietnam war mediation, 190, 193

Wilson, Woodrow, 54, 55, 66-73
Women's League for Peace and Freedom, 98, 99. *See also* Women's Peace Party
Women's Peace Party, 96
World War I, 49, 65, 66, 68-70, 79, 97, 115-16, 133
World War II, 55, 103, 110-11, 116, 135-36

Young, Owen D., 84